Build Full Stack NextJs AI SAAS App

Greg Lim

Copyright © 2025 Greg Lim
All rights reserved.

COPYRIGHT © 2025 BY GREG LIM

ALL RIGHTS RESERVED.
NO PART OF THIS BOOK MAY BE REPRODUCED IN ANY FORM OR BY ANY ELECTRONIC OR MECHANICAL MEANS INCLUDING INFORMATION STORAGE AND RETRIEVAL SYSTEMS, WITHOUT PERMISSION IN WRITING FROM THE AUTHOR. THE ONLY EXCEPTION IS BY A REVIEWER, WHO MAY QUOTE SHORT EXCERPTS IN A REVIEW.

FIRST EDITION: JANUARY 2025

Table of Contents

PREFACE 5

Chapter 1: Introduction 7

Chapter 2: Project Setup 13

Chapter 3: Backend Setup 21

Chapter 4: Authentication 31

Chapter 5: Dashboard 57

Chapter 6: Form UI 69

Chapter 7: Generate Interior Design with AI 97

Chapter 8: Custom Loading 123

Chapter 9: Display Output 126

Chapter 10: Display User's Images 137

Chapter 11: Payment Gateway 147

Chapter 12: Deploy App 165

ABOUT THE AUTHOR 175

PREFACE

About this book

In this book, we take you on a fun, hands-on and pragmatic journey to learning how to build full stack NextJs AI SAAS apps. You'll start building within minutes. Every chapter is written in a bite-sized manner and straight to the point as I don't want to waste your time (and most certainly mine) on the content you don't need. In the course of this book, we will cover:
- Chapter 1: Introduction
- Chapter 2: Project Setup
- Chapter 3: Backend Setup
- Chapter 4: Authentication
- Chapter 5: Dashboard
- Chapter 6: Form UI
- Chapter 7: Generate Interior Design with AI
- Chapter 8: Custom Loading
- Chapter 9: Display Output
- Chapter 10: Display User's Images
- Chapter 11: Payment Gateway
- Chapter 12: Deploy App

The goal of this book is to teach you in a manageable way without overwhelming you. We focus only on the essentials and cover the material in a hands-on practice manner for you to code along.

Requirements

You should have basic programming knowledge. But if you have some React or NextJs experience, it will be very helpful. Contact support@i-ducate.com to receive a copy of my NextJs introductory book.

Getting Book Updates

To receive updated versions of the book, subscribe to our mailing list by sending a mail to support@i-ducate.com. I try to update my books to use the latest version of software, libraries and will update the codes/content in this book. So, do subscribe to my list to receive updated copies!

Code Examples

You can obtain the source code of the completed project by contacting support@i-ducate.com

Build Full Stack NextJs AI SAAS

Chapter 1: Introduction

In this book, we will build an AI room and home interior design application using React, Next.js, and AI. In this full-stack application, we'll learn how to transform any room into a beautiful interior space with the help of AI.

Let's first walk through the application, and then we'll discuss the tech stack we'll use to build it. On the landing screen, you'll see how AI can elevate your room's interior to a new level.

When you click on 'Get Started', you'll be directed to the login or signup screen.

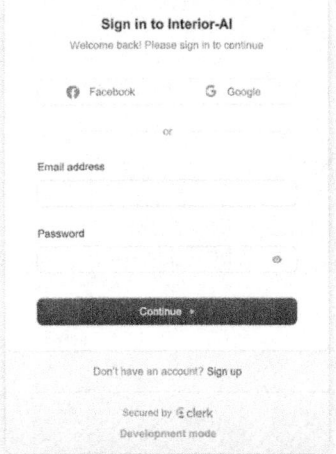

Build Full Stack NextJs AI SAAS

We will use both social authentication and email/password authentication. Once you log into the app, you'll be redirected to the dashboard. At the top, you can view your available credits and the user profile section:

There's an option to purchase more credits:

Clicking on 'Generate AI Interior' will take you where you can upload an image of your room:

To change the interior of this particular room, select the room type - whether it's a bedroom, kitchen, or office, and choose an interior design style.

If you have any specific requirements, you can specify in 'Enter Additional Requirements':

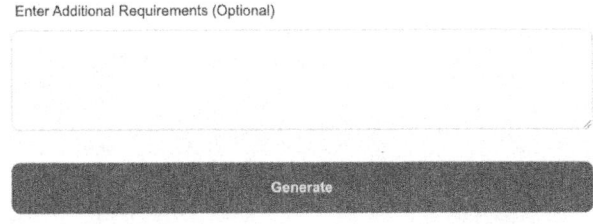

When you click 'Generate', a loading indicator will appear and we'll wait for the AI to generate the interior design for your room. Once the image is ready, you'll see both the original image and the AI-generated design side by side in a slider which you can drag to the left and right for comparison:

Generating an AI image uses one credit, and you'll see your credit balance subtract by one accordingly:

Back in the dashboard, you can see your AI generated room design displayed. The dashboard is where you can view all your previous AI generations. We store each image on a server, ensuring you can access your designs anytime:

If you need more credits, simply click the "Buy More Credits" option at the top:

When you land on this page, you'll see options to select the number of credits you want to add to your account:

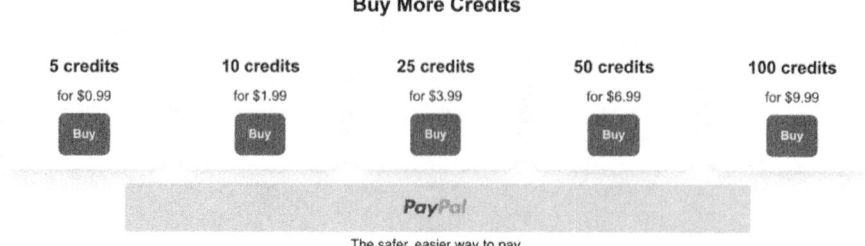

Let's say you want to select 25 credits, which costs $3.99. Once selected, the PayPal payment gateway will activate. You can choose to pay either through PayPal or with a debit/credit card.

This is a complete SaaS application with integrated PayPal payments - allowing you to start monetizing right away. We will guide you through the complete workflow and show you how to integrate the PayPal payment gateway.

This is a full-stack application, and it would be great if you have some basic experience with React or Next.js. But if not, you should still be able to get by this book, although it would be a greater challenge. I have a beginner's Next.js book that you can get by contacting support@i-ducate.com.

Tech Stack

For this application's tech stack. we'll use the React framework Next.js. For the database, we'll use Neon PostgreSQL along with Drizzle ORM, which allows you to perform CRUD operations seamlessly.

For authentication, we'll use Clerk Authentication, which is easy to integrate and provides multiple authentication options like email and social media accounts. We'll use Firebase Storage to store our images and assets.

We'll use Replicate.com to access AI APIs. To access this project's entire source code, drop a mail to support@i-ducate.com.

Let's move on to the next chapter to set up our project!

Chapter 2: Project Setup

For those new to Next.js, we'll build everything from scratch. First, go to *nextjs*.org and navigate to the *docs* section. There you'll find installation instructions.

Navigate to the folder where you want to create your Next.js application. Open a terminal in that folder (or Command Prompt if you're using Windows). Run the command:

```
npx create-next-app@latest
```

This command will install the latest version of Next.js.

Press Enter, and when asked "Do you want to proceed?", type "yes". Next, provide your project name - in this case, let's use "interior-ai " and press Enter:

```
(base) MacBook-Air-4:saasbook user$ npx create-next-app@latest
Need to install the following packages:
create-next-app@15.1.3
Ok to proceed? (y)
✓ What is your project named? … interior-ai
```

For the following prompts:
- Would you like to use TypeScript? → Select "no" (we won't be using TypeScript in this tutorial)
- Would you like to use ESLint? → Select "no"
- Would you like to use Tailwind CSS? → Select "yes"

```
✓ What is your project named? … interior-ai
✓ Would you like to use TypeScript? … No / Yes
✓ Would you like to use ESLint? … No / Yes
✓ Would you like to use Tailwind CSS? … No / Yes
✓ Would you like your code inside a `src/` directory? … No / Yes
✓ Would you like to use App Router? (recommended) … No / Yes
✓ Would you like to use Turbopack for `next dev`? … No / Yes
✓ Would you like to customize the import alias (`@/*` by default)? … No / Yes
Creating a new Next.js app in /Users/user/saasbook/interior-ai.
```

For the remaining prompts:
- Would you like to use src/ directory? → Select "no"
- Would you like to use App Router? → Select "yes"
- Would you like to customize the default import alias? → Select "no"

The installer will then begin downloading dependencies including React, React DOM, Next.js, PostCSS, and Tailwind CSS. Once installation is complete and you see the success message, open VS Code (the recommended IDE we will use in this book), navigate to and open the project folder you just created.

Before we proceed, search for and install the 'React Redux Snippets' VS Code extension:

The React Redux snippet tool will provide code suggestions and help you write code more efficiently by importing default templates. We will see this in action later.

Folder Structure Walkthrough

Let's first explore the folder structure. The most important directory is the *app* folder, where we'll write all our routing, components, and code:

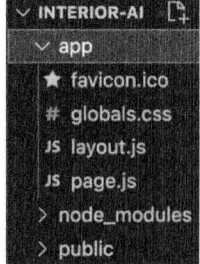

Inside, you'll find:
- *global*.css: contains CSS styles that apply throughout your application
- *layout*.js: holds your application's layout structure. Every Next.js application requires at least one layout file, known as the root layout
- *page*.js: your application's default page, which renders when you first run the application.

Inside /*app*/*layout*.js, you'll find HTML and body content that renders the children components.

```js
import { Geist, Geist_Mono } from "next/font/google";
import "./globals.css";

const geistSans = Geist({
  variable: "--font-geist-sans",
  subsets: ["latin"],
});

const geistMono = Geist_Mono({
  variable: "--font-geist-mono",
  subsets: ["latin"],
});

export const metadata = {
  title: "Create Next App",
  description: "Generated by create next app",
};

export default function RootLayout({ children }) {
  return (
    <html lang="en">
      <body
        className={`${geistSans.variable} ${geistMono.variable} antialiased`}
      >
        {children}
      </body>
    </html>
  );
}
```

There's also metadata configuration to help with SEO for your pages, and you'll notice the local font implementation.

Other important files include:
- *.gitignore*: specifies which files to exclude when pushing to GitHub
- *next.config*.js: contains Next.js-specific configurations
- *package*.json: includes:
    o Scripts for running and building your application
    o Project dependencies
    o Project metadata (name and version)
- *postcss.config*.js and *tailwind.config*.js: handle Tailwind CSS configuration

Don't worry too much about these files for now. We will revisit them when needed as we progress along this book.

To run the application, in the terminal, cd to the 'interior-ai' folder, run:

```
npm run dev
```

```
(base) MacBook-Air-4:saasbook user$ cd interior-ai/
(base) MacBook-Air-4:interior-ai user$ npm run dev

> interior-ai@0.1.0 dev
> next dev

  ▲ Next.js 15.1.3
  - Local:        http://localhost:3000
  - Network:      http://172.21.15.30:3000

 ✓ Starting...
 ✓ Ready in 2.7s
```

This will start your application on *localhost:3000*. Open this URL in your web browser to see the default Next.js application running:

In VS Code, navigate to *page*.js, which is your default page file. Whatever code is written here will be displayed on the screen. Let's remove all the default content and replace it with a simple "Hello World" example (shown below):

```
import React from 'react'

function Home() {
  return (
    <div>Home</div>
  )
}
export default Home
```

When you save the file, you'll see the changes immediately rendered in the browser:

Home

Thanks to hot reload functionality, you don't need to manually refresh – code changes automatically reflect as you save. This makes development much more efficient.

Next, we'll install DaisyUI, a plugin for Tailwind CSS that provides a collection of pre-built components and utility classes. It helps you build user interfaces more quickly while still using Tailwind's utility-first approach. Go to *daisyui*.com:

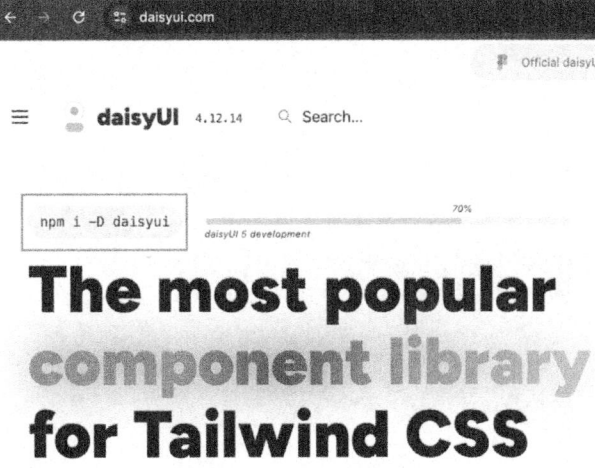

Copy the provided *npm* command:

```
npm i -D daisyui@latest
```

In a new Terminal, navigate to your project folder and run the command to integrate DaisyUI into your Next.js project.

Next, add daisyUI to *tailwind.config.js* in your project:

```
export default {
  ...
  plugins: [
    require('daisyui'),
  ],
};
```

To use DaisyUI components, scroll through the DaisyUI documentation to browse available components such as, Buttons, Navbar, Cards and many others:

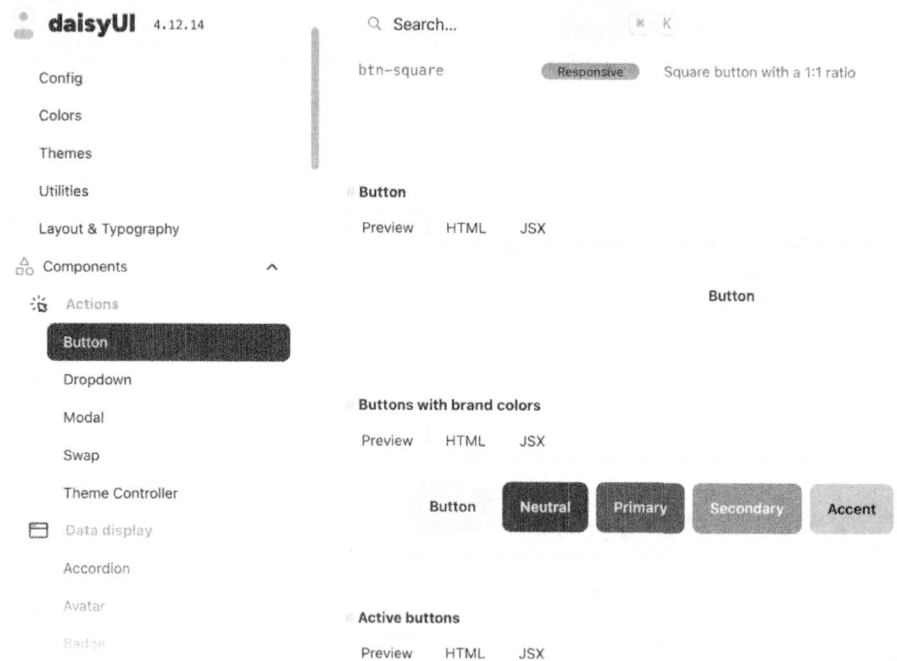

To use any component, copy its JSX code. For example, to use the button component:

Copy its JSX code and in */app/page*.js, paste it in your code as shown in **bold**:
...

```
function Home() {
  return (
    <div>
      <button className="btn">Button</button>
    </div>
  )
}
```
...

When you save the changes, you'll see a beautifully styled button appear:

Thanks to DaisyUI, all styling is handled automatically - no additional CSS needed. You can choose between different button styles. For e.g.:

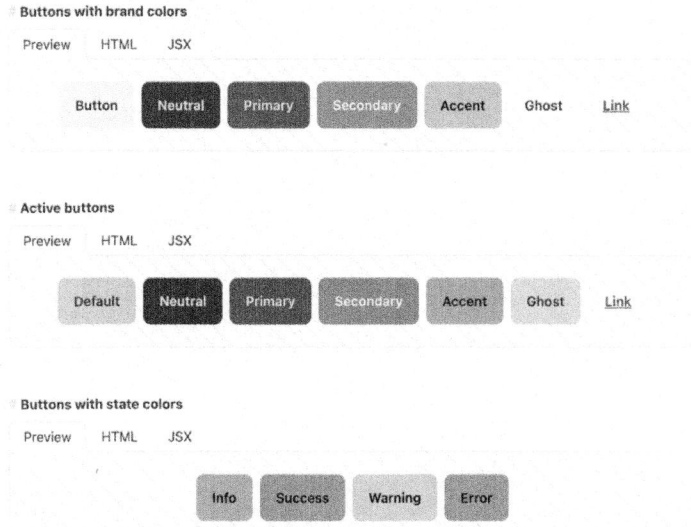

Next, for simplicity and to focus on the Saas aspects in this book, let's remove the font related code from *layout*.js. *layout*.js will thus just consist of:

```
import "./globals.css";

export const metadata = {
  title: "Create Next App",
  description: "Generated by create next app",
};

export default function RootLayout({ children }) {
  return (
    <html lang="en">
      <body>
        {children}
      </body>
    </html>
  );
}
```

In the next chapter, let's setup our backend.

Chapter 3: Backend Setup

For our application's backend, we'll use Drizzle ORM with Neon PostgreSQL database. Drizzle ORM makes implementing CRUD operations easier and performs faster than other ORMs currently available. To get started, visit *orm.drizzle.team*. Click "Get Started":

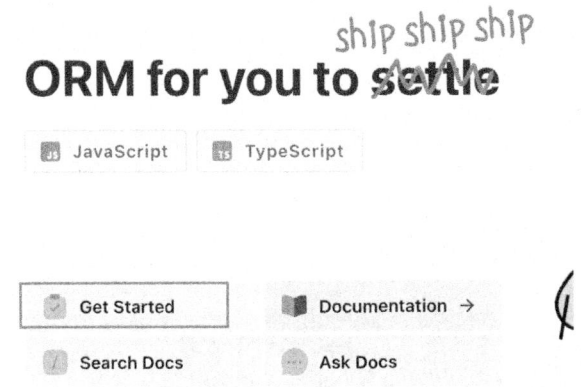

Select PostgreSQL Neon as your database:

We'll use Neon PostgreSQL to manage all our database records.

For installation, execute the following steps from the documentation. But note that we might modify them slightly since we're using JavaScript instead of TypeScript.

Step 1 – Install @neondatabase/serverless package

Return to your terminal and run the commands:
```
npm i drizzle-orm @neondatabase/serverless dotenv
npm i -D drizzle-kit
```

This will install, Drizzle ORM for Neon database server, dotenv package and Drizzle Kit.

Step 2 – Setup connection variables

After installation completes, in the root of our project, create a *.env* file to store your database URL (and other environment variables later on).

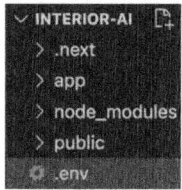

To get your database URL, go to *neon.tech* and log in (create an account if you don't have one):

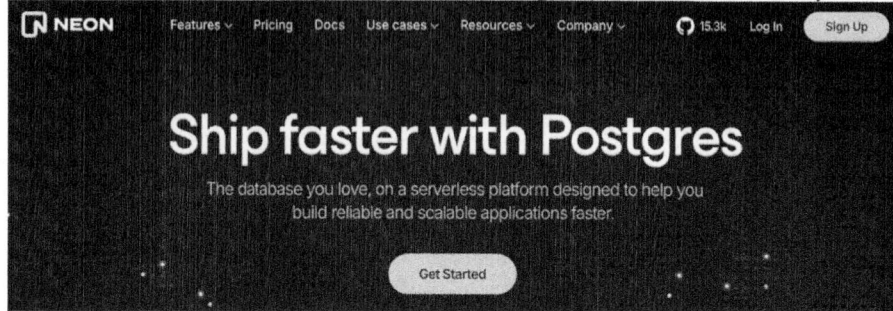

Access the Neon dashboard and create a new project:

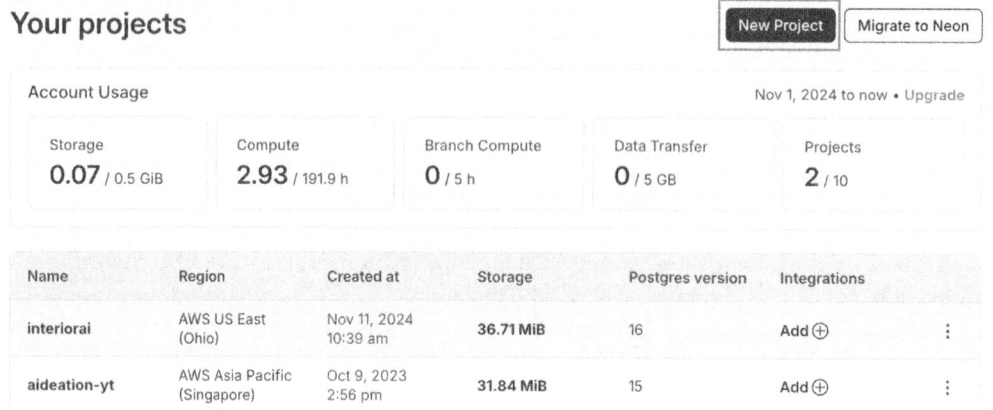

Name your project (e.g., "interior-ai") and click "Create" to set up your database with the default account settings:

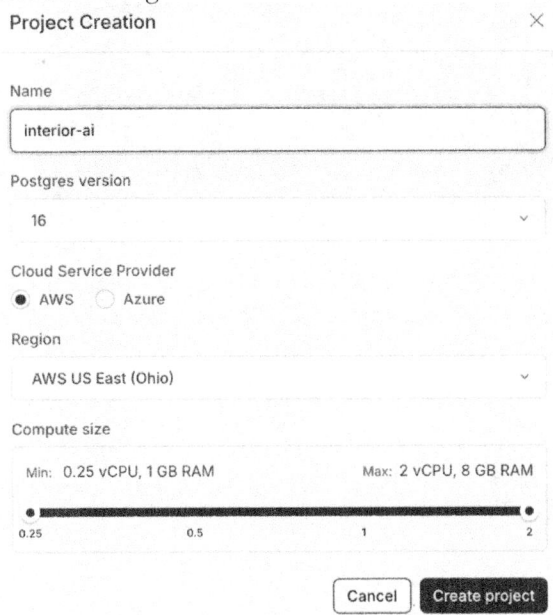

Within seconds, your connection string will be ready to use:

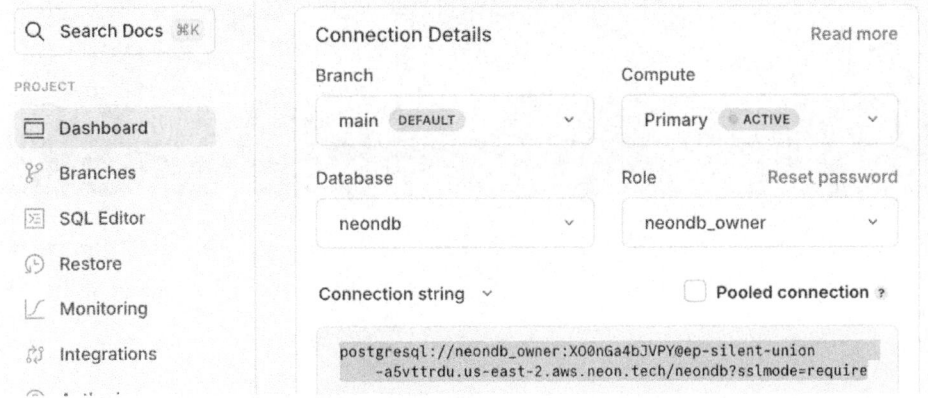

Copy the connection string, return to your application and paste it in your *.env* file:

NEXT_PUBLIC_DATABASE_URL=your_connection_string_here

E.g.:
NEXT_PUBLIC_DATABASE_URL=postgresql://neondb_owner:NI54ClyLAsHU@ep-broad-tooth-a5e4ywe7.us-east-2.aws.neon.tech/interior-ai?sslmode=require

Important: In Next.js, any environment variables that need to be accessed on the client side must start with *NEXT_PUBLIC_*. That's why we have **NEXT_PUBLIC**_*DATABASE_URL* instead of just *DATABASE_URL*.

Step 3 – Connect Drizele ORM to the database

In your application root, create a new folder called *config*. In it, create a file named *db*.js and paste the code:

```
import { drizzle } from 'drizzle-orm/neon-http';
export const db = drizzle(process.env.NEXT_PUBLIC_DATABASE_URL);
```

We export the database reference, and passed the NEXT_PUBLIC_DATABASE_URL environment variable key in. After exporting, this configuration will be available throughout your application.

Step 4 - Schema File

Next, we need to create a schema file. In our *config* folder, create our *schema*.js file and add the table definition:

```
import { pgTable } from 'drizzle-orm/pg-core'

export const Users = pgTable('users', {

});
```

```
EXPLORER                JS schema.js ×
∨ INTERIOR-AI           config > JS schema.js > ...
  > .next                1    import { pgTable } from 'drizzle-orm/pg-core'
  > app                  2
  ∨ config               3  ∨ export const Users = pgTable('users', {
    JS db.js             4
    JS schema.js         5    });
```

A schema defines your database tables and their columns, which we'll reference throughout our application. Let's create the *users* table with its columns by adding in **bold**:

```
import { pgTable, serial, varchar, integer } from 'drizzle-orm/pg-core'
export const Users = pgTable('users', {
  id: serial('id').primaryKey(),
  name: varchar('name').notNull(),
  email: varchar('email').notNull(),
  imageUrl: varchar('image_url').notNull(),
  credits: integer('credits').default(3)
});
```

Code Explanation

In this schema, we have columns:

- *id*: Auto-incrementing primary key (1, 2, 3, ...)
- *name*: Required text field
- *email*: Required text field
- *imageUrl*: Required text field for user's profile image
- *credits*: Required integer field for user's credit balance (with default value of 3)

All the column types are imported from *pg-core* (*pg* stands for Postgres):

```
import { pgTable, serial, varchar, integer } from 'drizzle-orm/pg-core'
```

After saving the schema, we need to update our database. But first, let's set up our *drizzle.config* file.

Step 5 - Setup Drizzle Config File

Step 5 - Setup Drizzle config file

Drizzle config - a configuration file that is used by Drizzle Kit and contains all the information about your database connection, migration folder and schema files.

Create a `drizzle.config.ts` file in the root of your project and add the following content:

```ts
// drizzle.config.ts
import 'dotenv/config';
import { defineConfig } from 'drizzle-kit';

export default defineConfig({
  out: './drizzle',
  schema: './src/db/schema.ts',
  dialect: 'postgresql',
  dbCredentials: {
    url: process.env.DATABASE_URL!,
  },
});
```

Create a new file called 'drizzle.config.js' in your root directory, copy the above code snippet (from the documentation) and paste it in:

```js
import 'dotenv/config';
import { defineConfig } from 'drizzle-kit';
export default defineConfig({
  schema: './config/schema.js',
  dialect: 'postgresql',
  dbCredentials: {
    url: process.env.NEXT_PUBLIC_DATABASE_URL,
  },
});
```

Make sure you specify *NEXT_PUBLIC_DATABASE_URL* like before:

```
import 'dotenv/config';
import { defineConfig } from 'drizzle-kit';
export default defineConfig({
  schema: './config/schema.js',
  dialect: 'postgresql',
  dbCredentials: {
    url: process.env.NEXT_PUBLIC_DATABASE_URL,
  },
});
```

We specify the path to our schema file, i.e. './*config*/*schema*.js' – this points to the *schema*.js file inside the *config* folder:

```js
import 'dotenv/config';
import { defineConfig } from 'drizzle-kit';
export default defineConfig({
  schema: './config/schema.js',
  dialect: 'postgresql',
  dbCredentials: {
    url: process.env.NEXT_PUBLIC_DATABASE_URL,
  },
});
```

Step 6 – Applying changes to the database

Our next step is to push the schema. Looking at the Drizzle ORM documentation, here's the command to push your changes:

Step 6 - Applying changes to the database

You can directly apply changes to your database using the `drizzle-kit push` command. This is a convenient method for quickly testing new schema designs or modifications in a local development environment, allowing for rapid iterations without the need to manage migration files:

```
npx drizzle-kit push
```

Run the command:

```
npx drizzle-kit push
```

The system will confirm by showing 'Pulling schema from database...' and 'Changes applied':

```
[✓] Pulling schema from database...
[✓] Changes applied
(base) MacBook-Air-4:interior-ai user$
```

To verify if everything is set up correctly, you can access your Neon dashboard and navigate to the *Tables* section, and you'll see the newly created 'users' table:

Build Full Stack NextJs AI SAAS

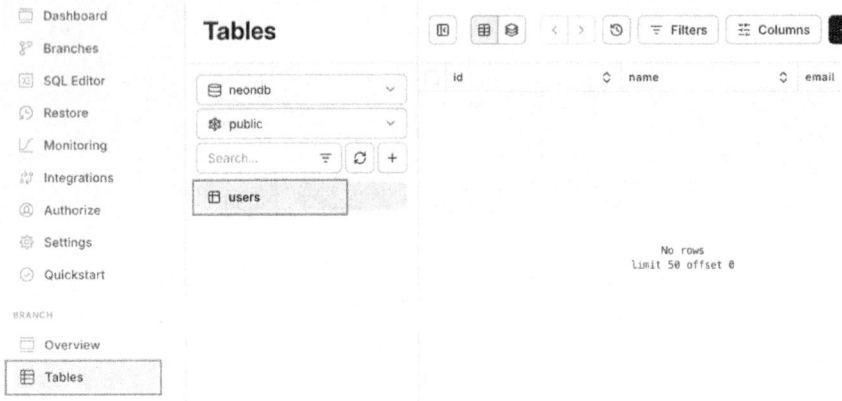

You should now see all the columns you defined in your schema:

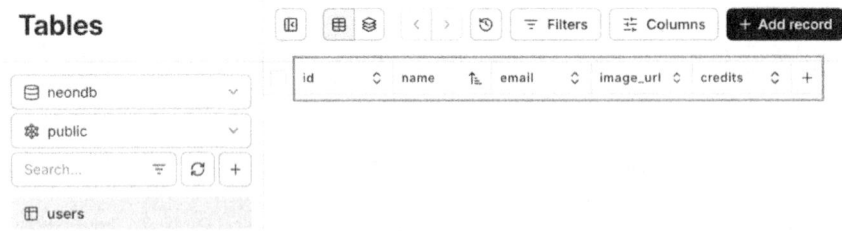

Using Drizzle Studio to Access your Database & Tables

Now that we've created the table and set up the backend for your application, let's explore another way to access your database and tables: Drizzle Studio. In the Drizzle documentation, you'll find a section called 'Studio'.

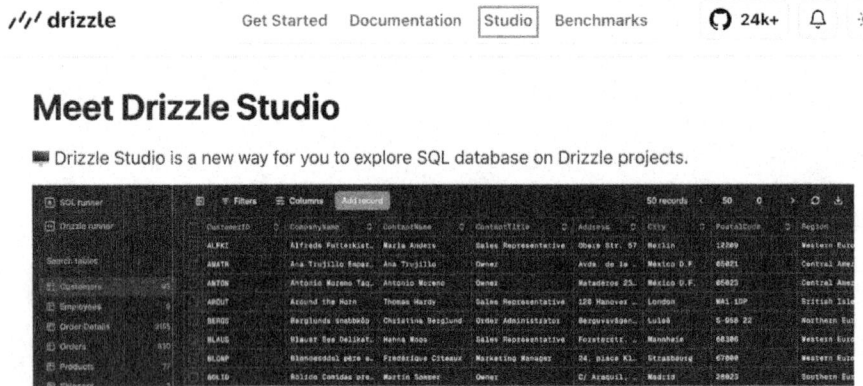

You can run Drizzle Studio on your local machine with:

```
npx drizzle-kit studio
```

Once you run the command, Drizzle Studio will start locally:

`Drizzle Studio is up and running on https://local.drizzle.studio`

Open the provided URL in your browser, and you'll see your database with the 'users' table displayed.

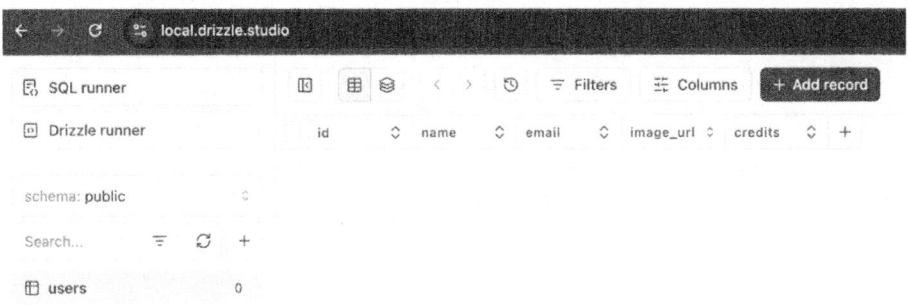

You'll find all the same features here that are available in the Neon dashboard. Additionally, Drizzle Studio offers the ability to run both SQL queries and Drizzle queries. If you click on the *schema* tab, you'll see the schema file we just created:

```
import { pgTable, uniqueIndex, serial, varchar, integer } from "drizzle-orm/pg-core"
import { sql } from "drizzle-orm"


export const users = pgTable("users", {
    id: serial("id").primaryKey().notNull(),
    name: varchar("name").notNull(),
    email: varchar("email").notNull(),
    imageUrl: varchar("image_url").notNull(),
    credits: integer("credits").default(sql`3`),
},
(table) => {
    return {
        pkey: uniqueIndex("users_pkey").on(table.id),
    }
});
```

With this, we've set up the backend for your application. You'll gain more hands-on experience as we develop the application further. When we start implementing database operations like adding and fetching records, you'll get a better understanding of how everything works together.

Chapter 4: Authentication

Let's implement authentication for our application. When users attempt to access the dashboard, we'll verify their authentication status. If a user is not authenticated, they will be redirected to the login/signup screen, where they can authenticate using Google, Facebook or email.

Once a user successfully authenticates, they will be redirected to the dashboard. For returning users who are already authenticated, they'll be automatically directed to the dashboard.

Let's return to our application. First, we'll create a new route for the dashboard. Inside the 'app' folder, create a new directory called 'dashboard', and within it, create a file named 'page.jsx'.

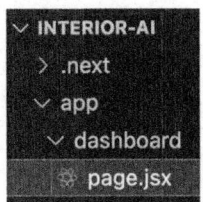

Use the 'rfce' snippet to generate a default React functional component template:

rcfe stands for React Function Export Component. Rename the component to 'Dashboard' as shown in **bold**:

```
import React from 'react'

function Dashboard() {
  return (
    <div>Dashboard</div>
  )
}

export default Dashboard
```

If we go back to *localhost:3000/dashboard*, you will see the new 'dashboard' route path rendered:

Dashboard

This shows how easily you can create a route in Next.js by simply adding a new folder.

Using Clerk for Authentication

For authentication, we'll be using Clerk (clerk.com):

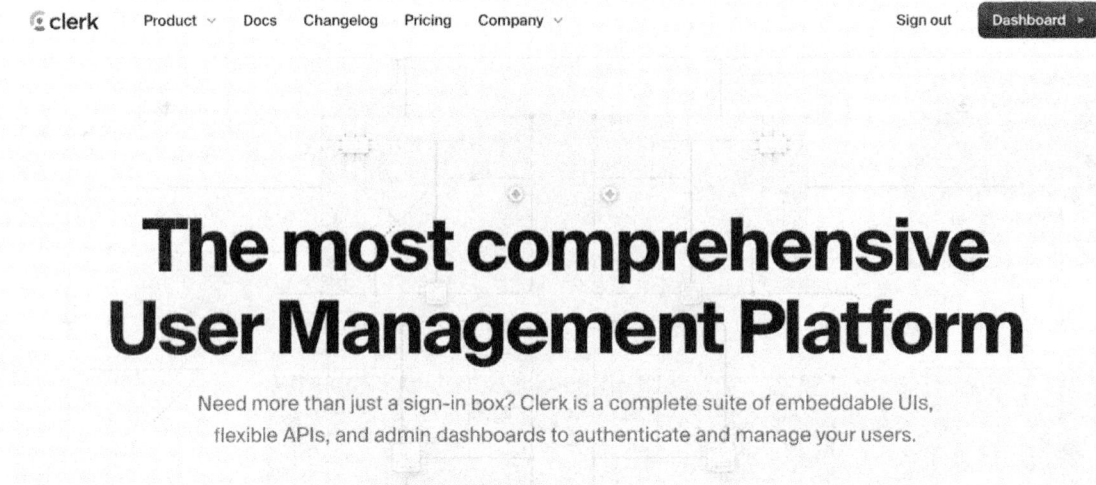

There are several reasons for this choice: First, Clerk is free to start using. Second, they provide a predefined UI kit, eliminating the need to write boilerplate code since Clerk handles that for you. Additionally, Clerk offers multiple authentication features including:

- Multi-factor authentication
- Email signup
- SMS authentication
- Password authentication
- Magic link login

They also provide various social authentication options and other security features.

To get started, go to clerk.com. If you don't have an account, create one and sign in - you'll be redirected to the dashboard. From there, you can create a new application:

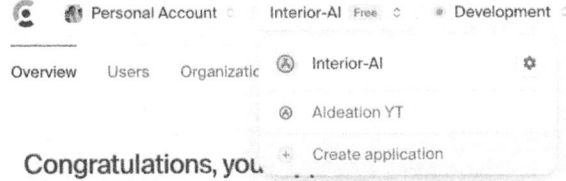

Click 'Create Application' and enter your application name – e.g., 'Interior-AI'. You can enable any sign-in options you want by toggling them:

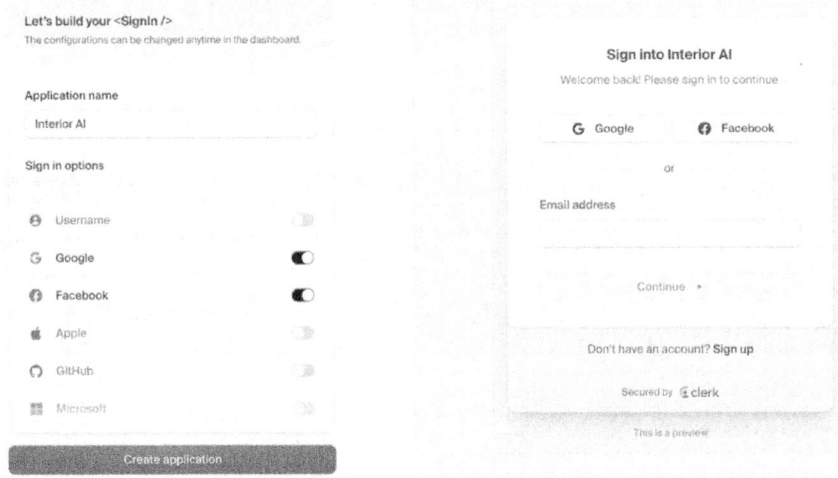

For example, if you want to enable Facebook login, toggle the Facebook option. The preview on the right-hand side shows how these options will appear on your screen. Click 'Create Application.' After creating the application, select the *Next.js* framework:

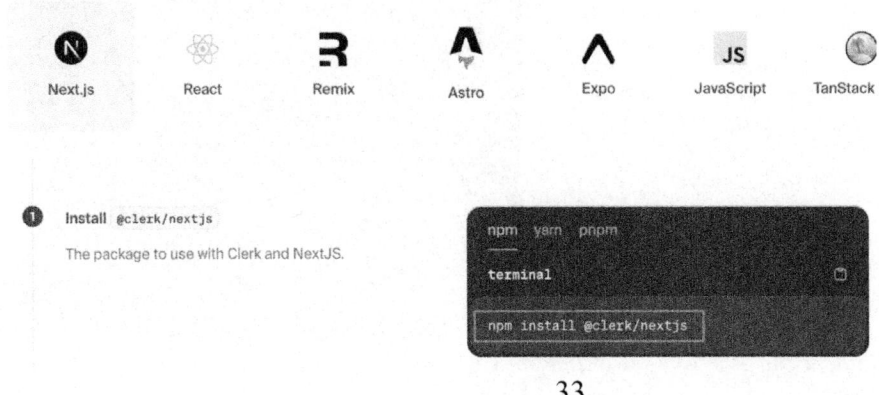

Run the command:

`npm install @clerk/nextjs`

to install Clerk in your Next.js application. Next, set the appropriate environment variables:

Copy these environment variable keys. Go to your project and in the *.env* file, paste the environment keys there - you'll need the Client Publisher Key and the Client Secret Key:

Note: Right now you are in development mode. When you move to production, you will need to change these keys.

Next, we need to create a *middleware*.ts file:

Create a new file called *middleware*.js in the project's root directory and paste the following code from

```js
import { clerkMiddleware } from "@clerk/nextjs/server";

export default clerkMiddleware();

export const config = {
  matcher: [
    // Skip Next.js internals and all static files, unle
    '/((?!_next|[^?]*\\.(?:html?|css|js(?!on)|jpe?g|webp
    // Always run for API routes
    '/(api|trpc)(.*)',
  ],
};
```

Currently, all routes are public. The documentation mentions the *clerkMiddleware* helper to configure protected routes.

3 Update `middleware.ts`

Update your middleware file or create one at the root of your project or `src/` directory if you're using a `src/` directory structure.

> The `clerkMiddleware` helper enables authentication and is where you'll configure your protected routes.

Go to 'clerk.com/docs/references/nextjs/clerk-middleware' (or Google 'clerkMiddleware'). Scroll down to find the section called 'Protect Routes':

Protect routes

You can protect routes by checking either or both of the following:

- **User authentication status** (user is signed in or out)
- **User authorization status** (user has the required role or permission)

35

```
auth.protect()    auth().userId()

middleware.ts

1  import { clerkMiddleware, createRouteMatcher } from '@clerk/nextjs/server'
2
3  const isProtectedRoute = createRouteMatcher(['/dashboard(.*)', '/forum(.*)'])
4
5  export default clerkMiddleware(async (auth, req) => {
6    if (isProtectedRoute(req)) await auth.protect()
7  })
```

The code changes are shown in **bold**:

```
import { clerkMiddleware, createRouteMatcher } from
'@clerk/nextjs/server'

const isProtectedRoute = createRouteMatcher(['/dashboard(.*)'])

export default clerkMiddleware(async (auth, req) => {
  if (isProtectedRoute(req)) {
    await auth.protect()
  }
})
export const config = {
  matcher: [
      ...
      ...
  ],
}
```

We import the Clerk middleware and *createRouteMatcher*. The dashboard route and all its child routes will be protected. Since we don't have a forum page, we can remove that route.

Next, return to the main documentation (clerk.com/docs/quickstarts/nextjs). We'll need to wrap our application in the Clerk Provider:

❹ Add `<ClerkProvider>` and Clerk components to your app

The `<ClerkProvider>` component wraps your app to provide active session and user context to Clerk's hooks and other components.

You can control which content signed-in and signed-out users can see with Clerk's **prebuilt control components**. Create a header using the following components:

- `<SignedIn>` : Children of this component can only be seen while **signed in**.
- `<SignedOut>` : Children of this component can only be seen while **signed out**.
- `<UserButton />` : Shows the signed-in user's avatar. Selecting it opens a dropdown menu with account management options.

```tsx
// app/layout.tsx
import { ClerkProvider, SignInButton, SignedIn, SignedOut, UserButton } from
import './globals.css'

export default function RootLayout({ children }: { children: React.ReactNode
  return (
    <ClerkProvider>
      <html lang="en">
        <body>
          <header>
            <SignedOut>
              <SignInButton />
            </SignedOut>
            <SignedIn>
              <UserButton />
            </SignedIn>
          </header>
          <main>{children}</main>
        </body>
      </html>
    </ClerkProvider>
  )
}
```

In /*app*/*layout*.js file, import *ClerkProvider* from *@clerk*/*nextjs* and wrap your content with it as shown in **bold**:

```
import "./globals.css";
import {
  ClerkProvider,
} from '@clerk/nextjs'

export const metadata = {
  title: "Create Next App",
  description: "Generated by create next app",
};

export default function RootLayout({ children }) {
  return (
    <ClerkProvider>
      <html lang="en">
        <body>
            {children}
        </body>
      </html>
    </ClerkProvider>
  );
}
```

Save the file and if you navigate to *localhost:3000/dashboard*, you'll see a sign-in page. However, this page is currently hosted on Clerk's domain rather than within our application:

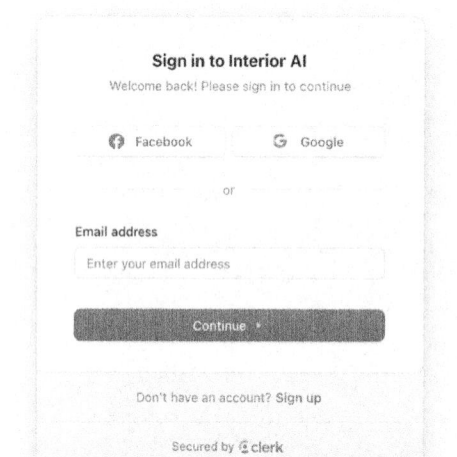

To keep users within our application, we have to create custom sign-in and sign-up pages. In the documentation, scroll down and click on this link:

Next steps

Utilize your own pages for authentication

The Account Portal is the fastest way to add authentication, but Clerk has pre-built, customizable components to use in your app too.

`Continue to the Next.js guide`

The documentation guides us on how to add the sign-up and sign-in pages. Copy the highlighted path for the sign-up page from the documentation:

❶ Build a sign-up page

The following example demonstrates how to render the `<SignUp />` component.

`app/sign-up/[[...sign-up]]/page.tsx`

First, in the *app* folder, create a '(auth)' folder in parentheses (brackets):

```
v app
  > (auth)
```

And in *(auth)*, create a new folder and paste the path you copied:

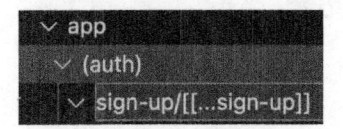

```
v app
  v (auth)
    v sign-up/[[...sign-up]]
```

Inside [*...sign-up*], create a *page*.jsx file:

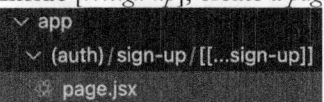

```
v app
  v (auth) / sign-up / [[...sign-up]]
      page.jsx
```

Copy and paste the documentation's code into the file as shown below:

❶ Build a sign-up page

The following example demonstrates how to render the `<SignUp />` component.

```tsx
// app/sign-up/[[...sign-up]]/page.tsx
import { SignUp } from '@clerk/nextjs'

export default function Page() {
  return <SignUp />
}
```

Repeat the same process for the sign-in page:

❷ Build a sign-in page

The following example demonstrates how to render the `<SignIn />` component.

```
app/sign-in/[[...sign-in]]/page.tsx
```

In the *(auth)* folder. Create the folder structure, and the *page*.jsx file:

Paste the code into *page*.jsx and save it:

```
app > (auth) > sign-in > [[...sign-in]] > page.jsx
1  import { SignIn } from '@clerk/nextjs'
2
3  export default function Page() {
4    return (
5      <SignIn />
6    )
7  }
```

In the next step 'Make the sign-up and sign-in routes public':

❸ Make the sign-up and sign-in routes public

By default, `clerkMiddleware()` makes all routes public. **This step is specifically for applications that have configured `clerkMiddleware()` to make all routes protected.** If you have not configured `clerkMiddleware()` to protect all routes, you can skip this step.

since we've already specified in *middleware*.js to protect the dashboard routes:

```
...
const isProtectedRoute = createRouteMatcher(['/dashboard(.*)'])
...
```

We can skip this step and move on to copy the environment variables:

❹ Update your environment variables

Update your environment variables to point to your cust more about the available environment variables.

```
.env.local
1  NEXT_PUBLIC_CLERK_SIGN_IN_URL=/sign-in
2  NEXT_PUBLIC_CLERK_SIGN_UP_URL=/sign-up
```

Navigate to the *.env* file and paste the variables:

```
NEXT_PUBLIC_DATABASE_URL=postgresql://neondb_owner:...
```

```
NEXT_PUBLIC_CLERK_PUBLISHABLE_KEY=pk_test_...
CLERK_SECRET_KEY=sk_test_vW1Uwz6E7y…
```

NEXT_PUBLIC_CLERK_SIGN_IN_URL=/sign-in
NEXT_PUBLIC_CLERK_SIGN_UP_URL=/sign-up

Navigate to *localhost:3000/dashboard*, and you'll see the sign-in UI kit rendered:

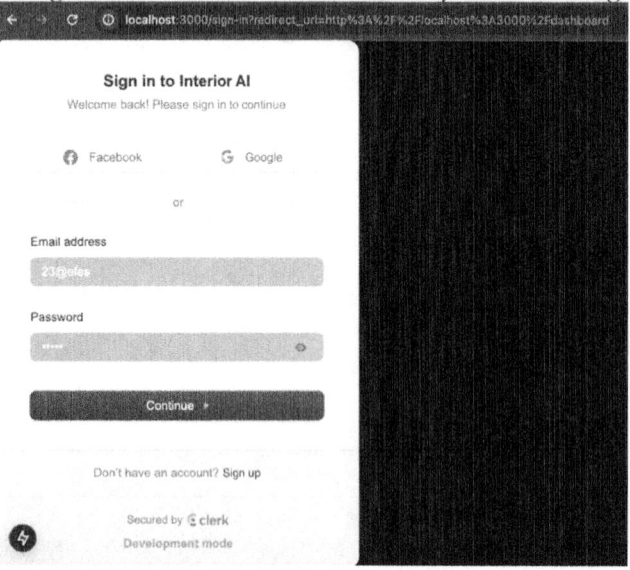

The authentication is now hosted on our domain.

Enchancing our Sign In Component

Currently, we have a basic *SignIn* component. Let's enhance it by wrapping the *SignIn* component inside a container div and adding CSS classes for centered alignment or whatever stylings you desire. In the SignIn component we created earlier, add in **bold**:

```
import { SignIn } from '@clerk/nextjs'

export default function Page() {
    return (
        <div className="min-h-screen flex items-center justify-center">
          <SignIn />
        </div>
    )
}
```

This centers your component on the screen. You can continue customizing the page with additional styling as needed:

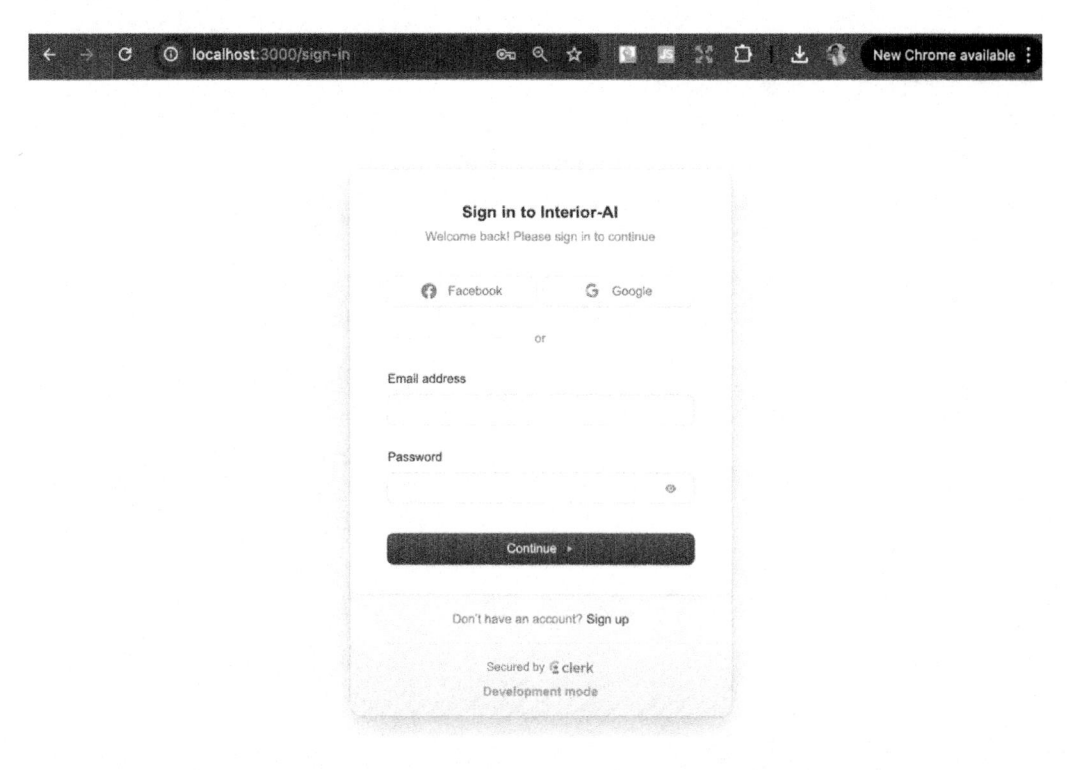

If you want to modify the sign-in card layout, visit the Clerk documentation and search for *Clerk Elements*:

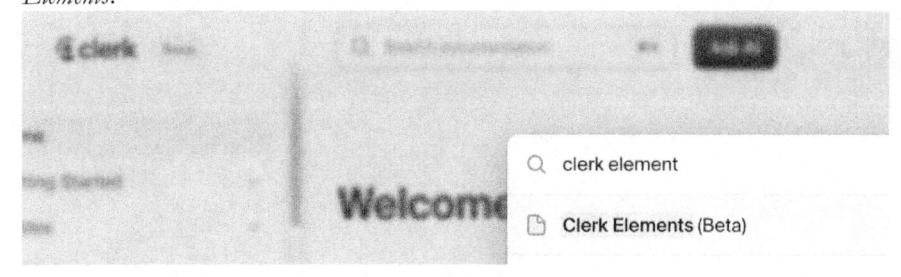

Clerk Elements is a new feature that provides pre-built components to help you create custom sign-in and sign-up components more efficiently.

Testing our App

Now, if you sign in with a Google/Facebook account, you'll be redirected to the dashboard page after successful authentication.

UserButton

Clerk provides a component called *UserButton* which displays a beautiful user profile item. In */app/dashboard/page*.jsx, let's add *UserButton* to our dashboard page by adding in **bold**:

```
import React from 'react'
import { UserButton } from '@clerk/nextjs'

function Dashboard() {
  return (
    <div>
      Dashboard
      <UserButton />
    </div>
  )
}

export default Dashboard
```

You will see the user profile icon. When you click on it, you'll see a menu with options to manage your account or sign out from the application:

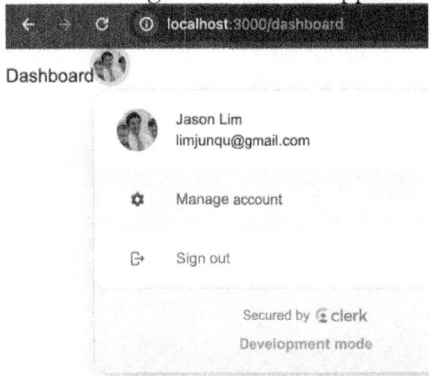

If you go to 'Manage Account', you'll have options to manage your profile. When you click 'Sign Out', you'll be redirected to the homepage. If you want to log in again, you'll be automatically redirected to the sign-in page.

Adding New Sign Up Users to the Database

When a user signs into our application, we want to add them to our database if they're new. For existing users, we'll check if they're already in our database. To implement this, create a new file inside the *app* folder called *provider*.js:

In Next.js, *provider*.js is commonly used as a wrapper component to set up and manage application-wide contexts that need to be accessible throughout your application. For e.g., in our case, we use it for database access, and later on PayPal payments. As we progress along, we will understand providers better.

In *provider*.js, add a default template and rename it to 'Provider'. We will also render its children. Here's the code:

```
import React from 'react'

function Provider({children}) {
  return (
    <div>{children}</div>
  )
}

export default Provider
```

In /*app*/*layout*.js, we'll import the *Provider* component and use it to render the children as shown in **bold**:

```
import { ClerkProvider } from '@clerk/nextjs'
import "./globals.css";
import Provider from "./provider";

...

export default function RootLayout({ children }) {
  return (
    <ClerkProvider>
      <html lang="en">
        <body>
          <Provider>
            {children}
          </Provider>
        </body>
      </html>
    </ClerkProvider>
  );
}
```

Currently, nothing will change visually - everything will remain the same. We're rendering these children through the *Provider* to enable sharing of data and functionality application wide.

Because this provider is having user interactions when they log in, the provider needs to run on the client side. Thus, add the 'use client' directive at the top of the file in */app/provider*.js:

```
"use client"
import React from 'react'

function Provider({children}) {
  return (
    <div>{children}</div>
  )
}

export default Provider
```

Next, when a user logs in, we need to verify them against our database. In *provider*.js, add in the codes in **bold**:

```
"use client"
import React, {useEffect} from 'react'
import { useUser } from '@clerk/nextjs'

function Provider({children}) {
  const {user} = useUser();

  useEffect(()=>{
     user&&VerifyUser();
  },[user])

  const VerifyUser = () => {
  }

  return (
       ...
  )
}
...
```

Code Explanation

```
const {user} = useUser();
```

We use the *useUser* hook from *@clerk/nextjs*, which provides us with the logged-in user's information.

```
useEffect(()=>{
   user&&VerifyUser();
},[user])
```

useEffect will call the *verifyUser* function when the *user* object is available and contains information:

```
const VerifyUser = () => {
}
```

We create a new method called *verifyUser* which we will implement soon.

Database API Call

Now we need to create a new API since we'll be making a database call and interacting with the database on the server side. Inside the *app* folder, create a new folder called 'api'. Inside this *api* folder, we'll create a new folder called 'verify-user' to create a new 'verify-user' endpoint:

```
v app
  > (auth)
  v api/verify-user
      route.jsx
```

In 'verify-user', create a *route*.jsx file and fill it with the following:
```
export async function POST(req){
  const {user} = await req.json();
}
```

We create an asynchronous function called POST that takes a request parameter. Inside this function, we receive the *user* object information in the request body from a POST API call. Next, let's return the response by adding:
```
import { NextResponse } from "next/server";

export async function POST(req){

  const {user} = await req.json();
  return NextResponse.json({'result':user})
}
```

We use *NextResponse.json()* to send back a result containing the user information in JSON format. This will confirm that we're successfully receiving the user data call to verify the user from within *provider*.js. Let's call the 'verify-user' api we just created. In *provider*.js, add in **bold**:

```
...
import { useUser } from '@clerk/nextjs'
import axios from 'axios';

function Provider({children}) {
  const {user} = useUser();

  useEffect(()=>{
     user&&VerifyUser();
  },[user])

  const VerifyUser = async() => {
     const dataResult=await axios.post('/api/verify-user',{
        user:user
     })

     console.log(dataResult.data)
  }
  ...
```

48

Code Explanation

First, we declare a *dataResult* constant and use *axios* to make the HTTP API call. Make sure you installed *axios* by running in the Terminal:

```
npm i axios
```

We use *await* with *axios.post()* to make a POST request to '/api/verify-user' which we defined previously in */app/api/verify-user*.

```
const dataResult=await axios.post('/api/verify-user',{
    user:user
})
console.log(dataResult.data)
```

We pass the *user* information as the request body by setting the body to 'user' and *console.log(dataResult.data)* to see the response.

Running our App

If you save and return to the browser, refreshing won't show any changes since we're not signed into the application. Navigate to the dashboard (*localhost:3000/dashboard*) and sign in by selecting your account. Once signed in, you'll see the user information in the console result:

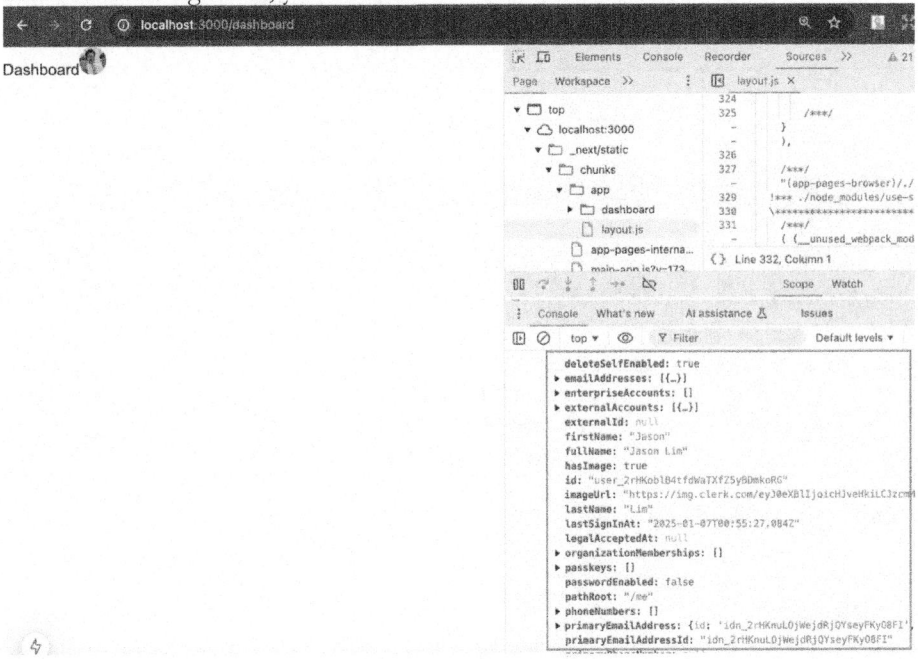

Right now in */api/verify-user/route.jsx*, we're just passing and returning the *user* information from the API call.

Next, we'll check if the user already exists in our database. If not, we'll add a new user. Let's wrap this logic in a try-catch block. Add in **bold**:

```
import { NextResponse } from "next/server";
import { db } from "../../../config/db";
import { Users }from "../../../config/schema";
import { eq } from "drizzle-orm";

export async function POST(req){
  const {user} = await req.json();

  try{
      const userInfo = await db.select().
                                from(Users).
                                where(
                                   eq(Users.email,
      user?.primaryEmailAddress.emailAddress)
                                             )
  }
  catch(e){
  }
  return NextResponse.json({'result':user})
}
```

Code Explanation

```
const userInfo = await db.
```

We create a constant called 'userInfo' that awaits a database query. We use the *db* reference we import from *config/db.js*, which contains our Drizzle ORM setup:

```
            const userInfo = await db.select().
                                      from(Users).
                                      where(
                                         eq(Users.email,
            user?.primaryEmailAddress.emailAddress)
                                                   )
```

Next in *.db*, we have:
- *.select()* fetches the database data.
- In *from*, we provide the 'Users' schema from *config/schema* as the source.

- In the *where* clause, with *eq()*, we check each row's email in our database table if it matches the user's primary email address that we receive from the request body in the API call back in *provider.js*:

```
const VerifyUser = async() => {
    const dataResult=await axios.post('/api/verify-user',{
        user:user
    })
    ...
}
```

Verify if User Exists

Save the changes and let's add a console.log to display *userInfo* to verify whether we're getting any results back from the database query. In */api/verify-user/route.jsx*, add in **bold**:

```
export async function POST(req){
  const {user} = await req.json();

  try{
      const userInfo = await db.select().
                                  from(Users).
                                  where(
                                      eq(Users.email,
      user?.primaryEmailAddress.emailAddress)
                                  )
      console.log("User:", userInfo);
  }
  catch(e){
  }
  return NextResponse.json({'result':user})
}
```

Let's check the terminal since the console output appears there, as this is running server-side. Looking at the console, we can see the *user* object is empty, which means this user doesn't exist in our database yet:

```
○ Compiling /api/verify-user ...
✓ Compiled /api/verify-user in 567ms (964 modules)
 GET /dashboard 200 in 44ms
User: []
 POST /api/verify-user 200 in 2215ms
```

Let's write a conditional check that if *userInfo.length* is empty (meaning the user doesn't exist), we'll save the user information. Add in the codes in **bold**:

```
    try{
        const userInfo = await db.select().
                                from(Users).
                                where(
                                    eq(Users.email,
                                    user?.primaryEmailAddress.emailAddres
                            s)
                                )

        console.log("User:", userInfo);

        if(userInfo?.length == 0){
            const SaveResult = await db.insert(Users).values({
                name: user?.fullName,
                email: user?.primaryEmailAddress.emailAddress,
                imageUrl: user?.imageUrl
            }).returning({Users})

            return NextResponse.json({'result':SaveResult[0].Users})
        }
        return NextResponse.json({'result':userInfo[0]})

    }catch(e){
        return NextResponse.json({error:e})
    }
```

Code Explanation

When *userInfo?.length* is empty (meaning the user doesn't exist), we use await *db.insert()* on the *Users* table, and in the values parameter, we'll pass all the user data, i.e. name, email, *imageUrl*.

```
            }).returning({Users})
```

After inserting, we use *.returning()* to return the newly inserted record after the insertion operation is completed. i.e. *SaveResult* will contain the complete user record that was just inserted into the database.

```
            return NextResponse.json({'result':SaveResult[0].Users})
```

We then return the complete user data as response. We need to specify [0] because SaveResult is an array and we access its first element.

```
    if(userInfo?.length == 0){
        ...
        return NextResponse.json({'result':SaveResult[0].Users})
    }
    return NextResponse.json({'result':userInfo[0]})
```

If the user already exists, return *NextResponse.json()* with *'result': userInfo[0]*.

```
}catch(e){
    return NextResponse.json({error:e})
}
```

In the *catch* block, we handle errors with (*e*).

In summary, if the user does not exist in the database, we add them. If the user already exists, it skips the *if* block and returns the existing user info.

Running our App

Let's save and run the application. Looking at the result now, we can see the complete user information being returned:

If we check Drizzle Studio and refresh, you'll see the new user record has been added:

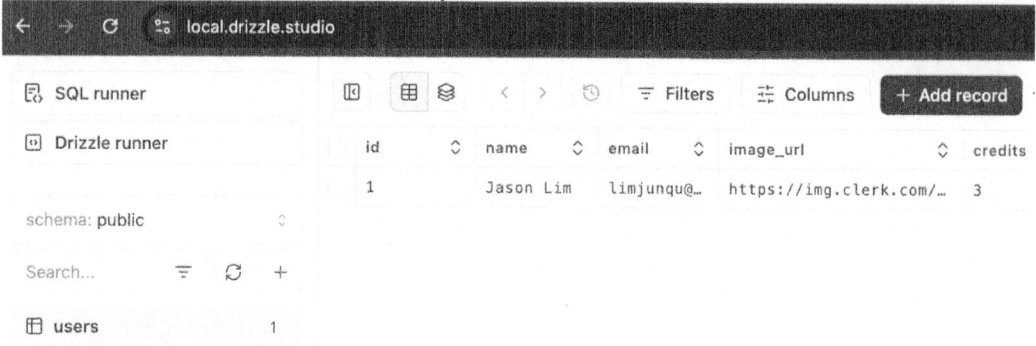

This demonstrates how we can insert a new record and verify if a user exists.

Now when we refresh, it returns the existing user data since it finds the user in the database and executes the *return* statement instead of the insert logic.

```
if(userInfo?.length == 0){
    const SaveResult = await db.insert(Users).values({
        name: user?.fullName,
        email: user?.primaryEmailAddress.emailAddress,
        imageUrl: user?.imageUrl
    }).returning({Users})

    return NextResponse.json({'result':SaveResult[0].Users})
}
return NextResponse.json({'result':userInfo[0]})
```

When it's a new user, it returns the newly inserted user.

Sharing the Logged-In User throughout the Application

Now that we've verified the user, we need to store their information so it can be shared throughout the application. This way, we won't need to make an API call every time user accesses a new page, and we'll have access to important fields like 'credits' that our application requires:

```
▼ {result: {…}} i
  ▼ result:
      credits: 3
      email: "limjunqu@gmail.com"
      id: 1
      imageUrl: "https://img.clerk.com/
      name: "Jason Lim"
    ▶ [[Prototype]]: Object
  ▶ [[Prototype]]: Object
```

To share this information across different components, we have two options: passing through props or using *Context*. *Context* is a powerful state management solution that helps share data across multiple components.

Under *app*, create a new folder called '_context' and inside it, create a file called 'UserDetailContext.jsx':

```
v app
  > _context
  > (auth)
  > api/verify-user
  > dashboard
```

We use an underscore prefix '_' for the *_context* folder name to tell Next.js not to treat this as a route, as it would automatically create a route for folders without underscores.

In *UserDetailContext*.jsx, add the codes:

```
import { createContext } from "react";

export const UserDetailContext=createContext();
```

Next, in *provider*.js, we wrap our application with *UserDetailContext.Provider* with the below codes in **bold**:

```
import React, { useEffect, useState } from 'react'
import { UserDetailContext } from './_context/UserDetailContext';
...
...
function Provider({children}) {

    const {user} = useUser();
    const [userDetail, setUserDetail] = useState([]);
    ...
    const VerifyUser = async() => {
        const dataResult=await axios.post('/api/verify-user',{
            user:user
        })
        setUserDetail(dataResult.data.result);
    }

    return (
     <UserDetailContext.Provider value={{ userDetail, setUserDetail }}>
       <div>{children}</div>
     </UserDetailContext.Provider>
  )
}
...
```

Code Explanation

```
const [userDetail, setUserDetail] = useState([]);
```

We define a *userDetail* state using *useState*, starting with an empty value.

```
const VerifyUser = async () => {
    const dataResult=await axios.post('/api/verify-user',{
        user:user
    })
    setUserDetail(dataResult.data.result);
}
```

When we receive user information, we update *userDetail* by setting it to *dataResult.data.result*.

```
<UserDetailContext.Provider value={{ userDetail, setUserDetail }}>
    <div>{children}</div>
</UserDetailContext.Provider>
```

We pass the *userDetail* state as a default value to the provider and wrap our application content inside it.

Now we're ready to use this context. Throughout the application, you can now access the user details by using **UserDetailContext**. We will illustrate this later.

This completes our setup of authentication, saving users to the database, and making user information accessible across the application.

Chapter 5: Dashboard

Let's implement the dashboard with these sections:
- Header section
- Welcome section that displays the username and provides a button to generate AI Interior
- Listing section to list the AI generated room images

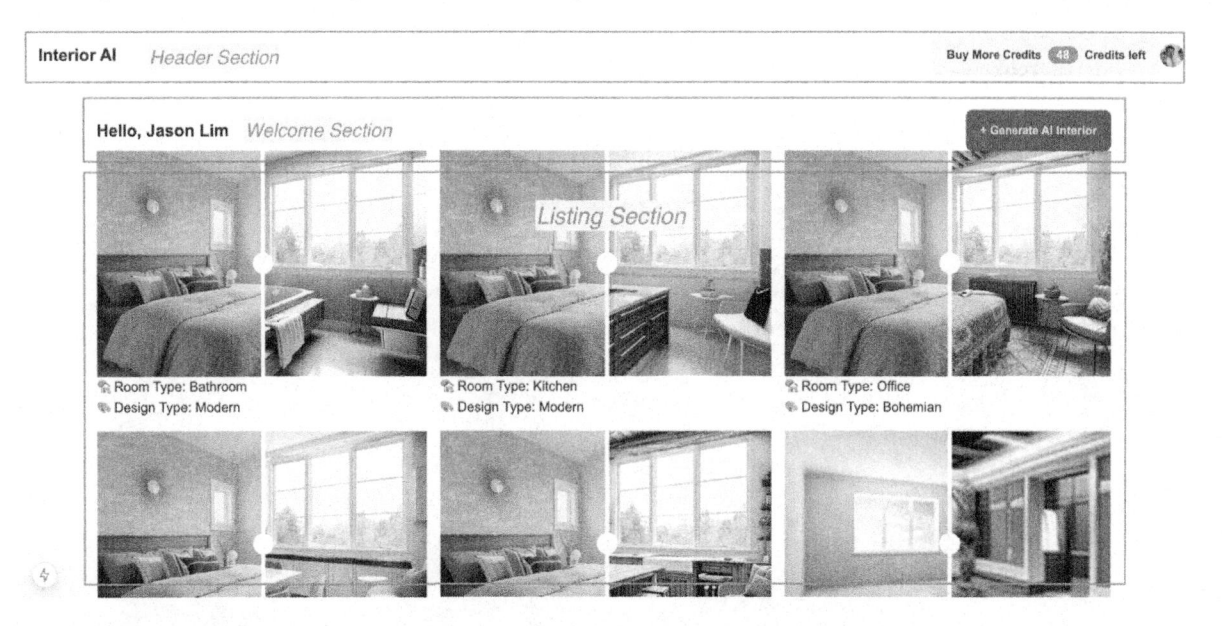

Inside the *dashboard* directory, create a layout file *layout.jsx*. Use a default 'rcfe' template and name it 'DashboardLayout':

This layout will be specific to the dashboard and render its children components. We add the *children* prop to handle nested content.

Let's add a header to our layout. Create a new folder called '_components' inside the *dashboard* directory - this will store all dashboard-related components. First, create the header component *Header*.jsx in this folder.

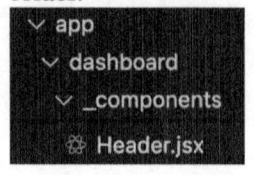

```
v app
  v dashboard
    v _components
        Header.jsx
```

Have a 'rcfe' default template, and save it:

```jsx
import React from 'react'

function Header({ children }) {
  return (
    <div>
      Header
    </div>
  );
}

export default Header
```

Then we'll import the header into our */dashboard/layout.jsx*:

```jsx
import React from 'react'
import Header from './_components/Header'

function DashboardLayout({ children }) {
  return (
    <div>
        <Header />
        {children}
    </div>
  );
}
...
```

Now, let's look at the app. The header will be visible:

localhost:3000/dashboard

Header
Dashboard

In the header, we want to add the app name on the left side:

Interior AI   Buy More Credits 48 Credits left

And on the right, we will have an option to buy more credits, display the user's available credit balance, and show the user's profile image.

We will use the Navbar component from DaisyUI for this. Go to daisyui.com/components/navbar/:

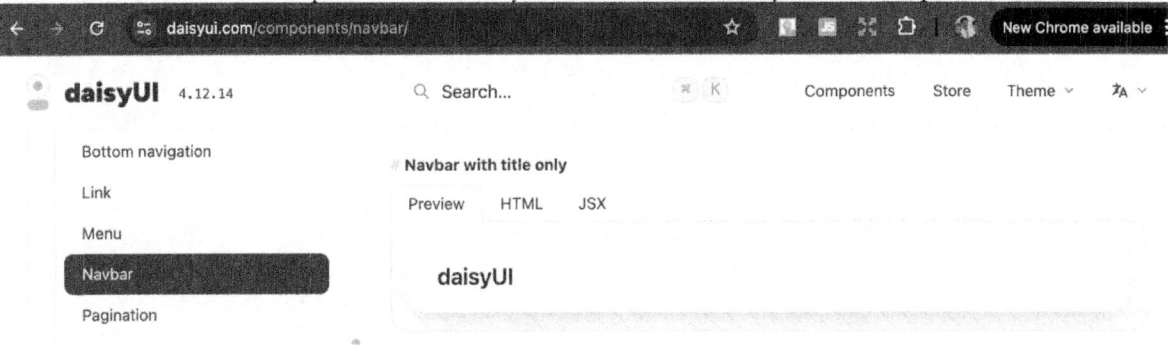

We will use the Navbar JSX code in */dashboard/_components/Header*.jsx. It will look something like the below in **bold**:

```
import React from 'react'

function Header() {

  return (
    <div className="navbar bg-base-100">
        <div className="flex-1">
            <a className="btn btn-ghost text-xl">Interior AI</a>
        </div>
    </div>
  )
}

export default Header
```

We changed the text to "Interior AI". You'll see "Interior AI" on the screen:

Interior AI

Dashboard

Next in *Header*.jsx, add a new div for the right-hand side content and in it, we'll add a *UserButton*. Add in **bold**:

```
"use client"
import React from 'react'
import { UserButton } from '@clerk/nextjs'

function Header() {

  return (
    <div className="navbar bg-base-100">
      <div className="flex-1">
        <a className="btn btn-ghost text-xl">Interior AI</a>
      </div>
      <div className="flex-none">
        <UserButton></UserButton>
      </div>
    </div>
  )
}
```

Because *UserButton* only works on the client side, so we convert *Header* to a client-side component by adding 'use client' at the top.

To position *UserButton* on the right, we added *flex-none*.

On the left side of *UserButton* (which shows our profile image), we'll display the user's available credits. We will use the *Badge* component from DaisyUI (daisyui.com/components/badge/):

In *Header*.jsx, add the following in **bold**:

```
function Header() {

  return (
    <div className="navbar bg-base-100">
      <div className="flex-1">
        <a className="btn btn-ghost text-xl">Interior AI</a>
      </div>
      <div className="flex-none">
        <button className="btn">
          <div className="badge badge-secondary">
            3
          </div>
          Credits left
        </button>
      </div>
      <div className="flex-none">
        <UserButton></UserButton>
      </div>
    </div>
  )
}
```

Now you can see the badge displaying the user's credits (currently hardcoded to 3):

Get Actual Credit

Currently, we've hardcoded the credit number, but we want to show the actual credits. To get this information, we'll use the *UserDetailContext* to access the database. In Header, add in the codes in **bold**:

```
"use client"
import React, { useContext } from 'react'
import { UserButton } from '@clerk/nextjs'
import { UserDetailContext } from '../../_context/UserDetailContext'

function Header() {
  const {userDetail,setUserDetail}=useContext(UserDetailContext);

  return (
    <div className="navbar bg-base-100">
      <div className="flex-1">
        <a className="btn btn-ghost text-xl">]Interior AI</a>
```

```
      </div>
      <div className="flex-none">
        <button className="btn">
          <div className="badge badge-secondary">
            {userDetail?.credits}
          </div>
          Credits left
        </button>
      </div>
      <div className="flex-none">
        <UserButton></UserButton>
      </div>
    </div>
  )
}
```

Code Explanation

```
const {userDetail,setUserDetail}=useContext(UserDetailContext);
```

First, define *userDetail* in curly braces, then use the *useContext* hook with *UserDetailContext*. Remember that *useContext* is a React Hook that allows us to share context values (e.g. user details) from a parent component anywhere in your component tree.

```
        <button className="btn">
          <div className="badge badge-secondary">
            {userDetail?.credits}
          </div>
          Credits left
        </button>
```

From *userDetail*, you can access the credits - it's showing three because that's what we have in our database. If we go to the database, you can see the value is three. Now, let's change it to five in *local.drizzle.studio*:

id	name	email	image_url	credits
1	Jason Lim	limjunqu@...	https://img.clerk.com/...	5

Save the changes and when you refresh the page, you can see it now shows five credits:

Interior AI   5 Credits left

This demonstrates how we can share information through context.

Listing Section

Now our header is complete. Next, we'll implement the Listing section component:

Go to the *_components* folder and create a new file for our Listing component, *Listing*.jsx:

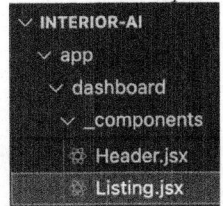

Give it a default template:
```
import React from 'react'

function Listing() {
  return (
    <div>Listing</div>
  )
}

export default Listing
```

In */dashboard/page*.jsx, import and render the *Listing* component:

```
import React from 'react'
import { UserButton } from '@clerk/nextjs'
import Listing from './_components/Listing'

function Dashboard() {
  return (
    <div>
      <UserButton />
      <Listing></Listing>
    </div>
  )
}

export default Dashboard
```

Note: we can remove *UserButton* since we are already rendering it in the Header.

When we return to the page, you'll see the listing. Let's add some padding and margin, by adding the codes in **bold** to */dashboard/layout*.jsx:

```
...
function DashboardLayout({ children }) {
  return (
    <div>
        <Header />
        <main className="p-4 md:p-6 lg:p-8 max-w-7xl mx-auto">
            {children}
        </main>
    </div>
  );
}
...
```

We wrap the *children* prop of the *DashboardLayout* component to apply the same styling to all routes rendered through this dashboard layout.

With `className="p-4 md:p-6 lg:p-8 max-w-7xl mx-auto"`, the content has progressively more padding as the screen gets larger and is centered. The layout thus adjusts to different screen sizes.

Let's return to /*dashboard*/*_components*/*Listing*.jsx. We will display the logged in user's name and a 'Generate' button. Fill it with the below codes:

```
"use client"
import { useUser} from '@clerk/clerk-react'
import React from 'react'

function Listing() {

  const {user} = useUser();

  return (
    <div>
        <div className="flex justify-between items-center text-xl font-bold">
            Hello, {user?.fullName}
            <button className="btn btn-primary">
                + Generate AI Interior
            </button>
        </div>
    </div>
  )
}

export default Listing
```

Code Explanation

```
  const {user} = useUser();
```

Create a constant called 'user' and set it equal to the *useUser* hook. Remember to convert this to a client component with `"use client"` because you're using client-side functionality i.e. the *useUser* hook from Clerk.

```
            Hello, {user?.fullName}
```

We display the logged in user's name using *user?.fullName*.

```
        <div className="flex justify-between items-center text-xl font-bold">
            Hello, {user?.fullName}
            <button className="btn btn-primary">
                + Generate AI Interior
            </button>
        </div>
```

We style it to make the font bold, large and placed the user name and button at opposite ends of the container.

Interior AI   5 Credits left

Hello, Jason Lim   + Generate AI Interior

Managing Generated Interiors Data

Let's next store the AI generated interiors when users create them. In *Listing*.jsx, add in the following codes in **bold**:

```
"use client"
import { useUser} from '@clerk/clerk-react'
import React, {useState} from 'react'

function Listing() {

  const {user} = useUser();
  const [userRoomList, setUserRoomList] = useState([]);

  return (
    <div>
        <div className="flex justify-between items-center text-xl font-bold">
            Hello, {user?.fullName}
            <button className="btn btn-primary">
                + Generate AI Interior
            </button>
        </div>
        {userRoomList?.length == 0 ?
            <div>
                No Interior AI Designs Generated Yet
            </div>
            :
            <div>

            </div>
        }
    </div>
  )
}

export default Listing
```

Code Explanation

```
const [userRoomList, setUserRoomList] = useState([]);
```

We create a state array for storing generated interior data.

```
{userRoomList?.length == 0 ?
    <div>
        No Interior AI Designs Generated Yet
    </div>
    :
    <div>

    </div>
}
```

We'll use conditional rendering: when *userRoomList* doesn't exist or its length is zero, we show a message **"No Interior AI Designs Generated Yet"**. Otherwise, we'll display a *div* with the listing.

Running our App

If we check now, **"No Interior AI Designs Generated Yet"** is showing because we don't have any listings or user rooms yet:

Interior AI

5 Credits left

Hello, Jason Lim

+ Generate AI Interior

No Interior AI Designs Generated Yet

We add the following stylings:

```
<div className="flex justify-center items-center h-full text-2xl text-gray-500 mt-32">
    No Interior AI Designs Generated Yet
</div>
```

This will align everything properly in a centered layout:

When users first visit the dashboard, they'll see this screen since they haven't created anything yet. They can start generating interiors by clicking the button. We will work on displaying generating interiors soon. But before that, we need to have a form to specify interior options before generation. Let's work on that in the next chapter.

Chapter 6: Form UI

When users click on '+ Generate AI Interior', they'll be redirected to a new route called 'Create New.' On this screen, users can upload an image of the room they want to redesign. They'll also have options to:
- select the room type from a dropdown menu (e.g. Living Room, Bedroom, Kitchen)
- choose a design style (e.g. modern, industrial)

It will look something like:

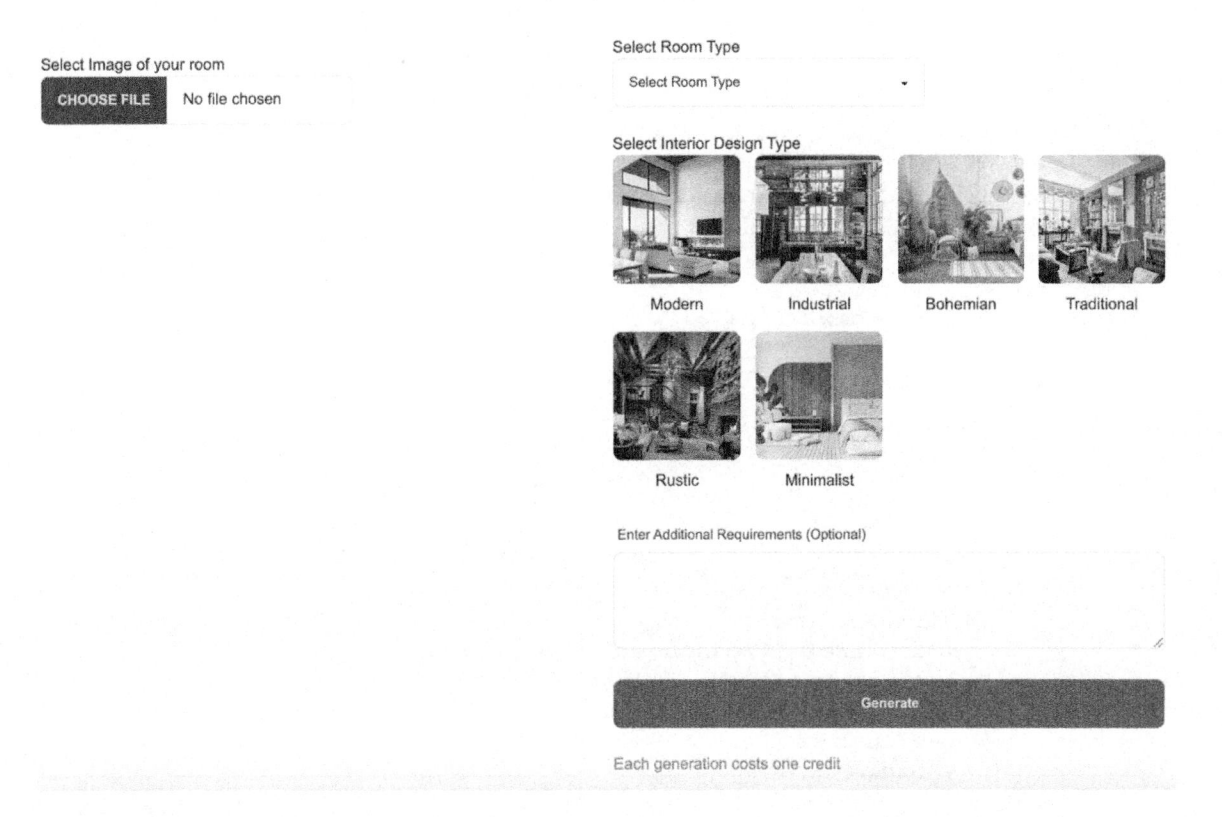

When you click 'Generate', our AI will begin working on redesigning the uploaded room.

Now, let's return to our application. First, we create a new route 'create-new' under the dashboard by creating a 'create-new' folder. Inside it, create a 'page.jsx' file:

```
 dashboard
  > _components
  v create-new
      page.jsx
```

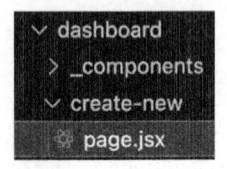

Fill it with default code:

```
import React from 'react'

function CreateNew() {
  return (
    <div>Create New</div>
  )
}

export default CreateNew
```

When a user clicks on the "+ Generate AI Interior" button, we want to redirect to the *create-new* page. In *Listing*.jsx, add in the codes in **bold**:

...
```
import React, {useState} from 'react'
import Link from 'next/link';

function Listing() {

  const {user} = useUser();
  const [userRoomList, setUserRoomList] = useState([]);

  return (
    <div>
        <div className="...">
            Hello, {user?.fullName}
            <Link href={'/dashboard/create-new'}>
              <button className="btn btn-primary">
                  + Generate AI Interior
              </button>
            </Link>
        </div>
...
...
```

We use the *Link* tag imported from 'next/link'. The *Link* component is equivalent to the anchor tag in HTML.

```
<Link href={'/dashboard/create-new'}>
```

Link requires an *href* attribute where you need to provide the path. In this case, the path is "dashboard/create-new". We simply wrap our button with this *Link* component.

Running our App

When we click on "+ Generate AI Interior", it now redirects to "dashboard/create-new", which currently displays the "Create New" text.

"Create New" Page

Let's implement the "Create New" page. Navigate to *dashboard/_components/create-new/page*.jsx file. We'll start by adding the text "Create AI Interior" as our heading. Add in **bold**:

```
"use client"
import React from 'react'

function CreateNew() {
  return (
        <div>
            <h2 style={{
                color: 'purple',
                fontWeight: 'bold',
                fontSize: '2.5rem', // Makes it much bigger
                textAlign: 'center' // Centers the text
            }}>
                Create AI Interior
            </h2>
        </div>
  )
}

export default CreateNew
```

We apply "use client" to *CreateNew* because it will contain several client slide form elements as we will see later on. You can see how the heading is displayed:

We next want to add an image upload option on the left side:

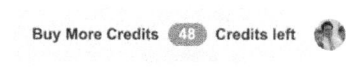

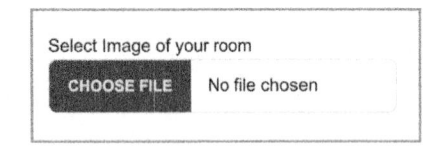

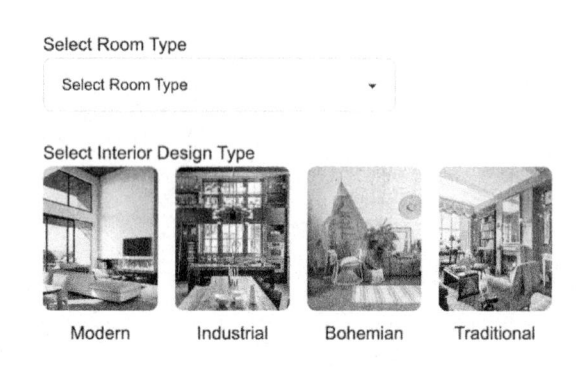

In *CreateNew*, let's add a div that will contain our image upload section by adding in **bold**:

```
"use client"
import React from 'react'
import ImageSelection from './_components/ImageSelection'

function CreateNew() {
  return (
      <div>
          <h2 style={{
              color: 'purple',
              fontWeight: 'bold',
              fontSize: '2.5rem', // Makes it much bigger
              textAlign: 'center' // Centers the text
          }}>
              Create AI Interior
```

```
        </h2>
        <div>
            <ImageSelection />
        </div>
      </div>
  )
}
```

Inside the *create-new* directory, let's create a new folder called *_components* to store all components related to this page:

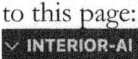

```
∨ INTERIOR-AI
  ∨ app
    ∨ dashboard
      ∨ create-new
        > _components
          page.jsx
```

_components will contain the *ImageSelection* component along with other form input sections. In *_components*, create *ImageSelection*.jsx and add a default template. We have imported this component into our *create-new* page previously.

Now we'll divide the Create New screen into two sections using *Grid*. In *…/create-new/page*.jsx, add:

```
function CreateNew() {
  return (
      <div>
          <h2 style={{
              color: 'purple',
              fontWeight: 'bold',
              fontSize: '2.5rem', // Makes it much bigger
              textAlign: 'center' // Centers the text
          }}>
              Create AI Interior
          </h2>
          <div className="grid grid-cols-2 gap-8 p-6">
             <div>
                <ImageSelection />
             </div>
          </div>
      </div>
  )
}
```

This would create a two-column layout where the columns have equal width, some space between them, and the entire grid has padding around its edges.

In .../createnew/_components/ImageSelection.jsx, fill in the below codes:

```
"use client"
import React from 'react'

function ImageSelection() {

  return (
    <div>
        <label>Select Image of your room</label>

        <div>
            <input type="file"
               accept="image/*"
               className="file-input file-input-bordered w-full max-w-xs"
            />
        </div>
    </div>
  )
}

export default ImageSelection
```

Code Explanation

We add a label that says "Select image of your room." Below that, we add a *File Input* taken from *daisyui.com/components/file-input/*:

```
            <input type="file"
               accept="image/*"
                className="file-input file-input-bordered w-full max-w-xs"
            />
```

We want to restrict users to selecting only image files, not other file types like PDFs, thus we add an *accept* parameter to only allow image files.

Handle File Selection

Let's implement a method to handle file selection. We'll create a function called *onFileSelected* that accepts an event parameter and console logs that targeted file. Add in **bold**:

```
function ImageSelection() {

  const onFileSelected = (event) =>{
    console.log(event.target.files[0])
  }

  return (
    <div>
        <label>Select Image of your room</label>

        <div>
            <input type="file"
                accept="image/*"
                className="file-input file-input-bordered w-full max-w-xs"
                onChange={onFileSelected}
            />
        </div>
    </div>
  )
}
```

We attach this method to our input using the *onChange* event handler. When you run the app now and select an image, in the developer console, you can see the file information logged:

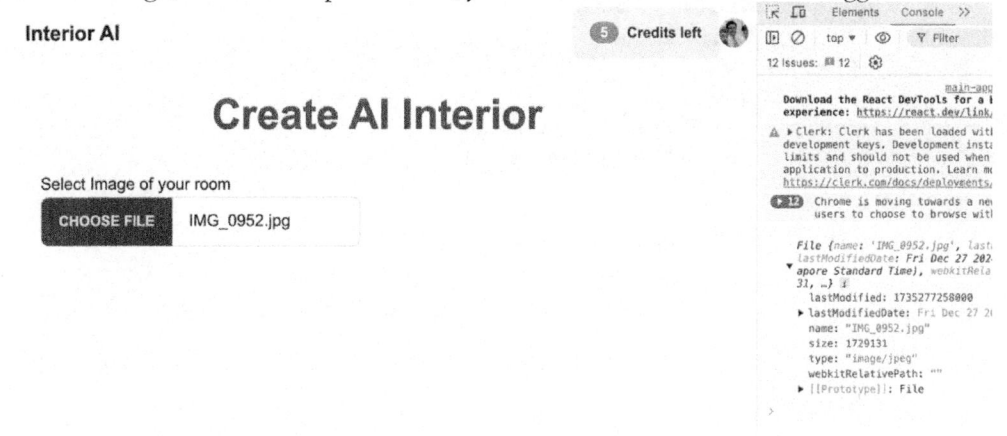

Show Preview of Selected Image

Now we want to show a preview of the selected file in our interface. Add the codes in **bold**:

```
"use client"
import React, {useState} from 'react'

function ImageSelection() {
  const [selectedImage, setSelectedImage] = useState(null);

  const onFileSelected = (event) =>{
    const file = event.target.files[0];
    if (file) {
        const imageUrl = URL.createObjectURL(file);
        setSelectedImage(imageUrl);
    }
  }
  return (
    <div>
        <label>Select Image of your room</label>
        <div>
            <input type="file"
                accept="image/*"
                className="file-input file-input-bordered w-full …"
                onChange={onFileSelected}
            />
        </div>
        {selectedImage && (
            <div style={{
                marginTop: '20px',
                maxWidth: '500px',
                width: '100%'
            }}>
                <img
                    src={selectedImage}
                    alt="Selected room"
                    style={{
                        width: '100%',
                        height: 'auto',
                        borderRadius: '8px',
                        boxShadow: '0 2px 8px rgba(0,0,0,0.1)'
                    }}
                />
            </div>
        )}
    </div>
  )
```

}

Code Explanation

```
"use client"
import React, {useState} from 'react'
```

We make this component client-side because we will use *useState* to store the selected file.

```
function ImageSelection() {
  const [selectedImage, setSelectedImage] = useState(null);

  const onFileSelected = (event) =>{
     const file = event.target.files[0];
     if (file) {
         const imageUrl = URL.createObjectURL(file);
         setSelectedImage(imageUrl);
     }
  }
```

We create an image file state. When a file is selected, we'll store it using *setSelectedImage(imageUrl)*.

Once a file is selected, we use *URL.createObjectURL(file)* which generates a temporary, unique URL that points to a file stored in the browser's memory. This URL can be used to display or reference the file, for our image preview.

```
         {selectedImage && (
              <div style={{
                  marginTop: '20px',
                  maxWidth: '500px',
                  width: '100%'
              }}>
                  <img
                       src={selectedImage}
                       alt="Selected room"
                       style={{
                           width: '100%',
                           height: 'auto',
                           borderRadius: '8px',
                           boxShadow: '0 2px 8px rgba(0,0,0,0.1)'
                       }}
                  />
              </div>
         )}
```

When an image file is selected, you can see the preview appears:

Interior AI

Create AI Interior

Select Image of your room

CHOOSE FILE   istockpho...2x612.jpg

Send Image File Back to Parent Component

When a file is selected, we need to send the file information back to the parent component. We'll create a prop called *selectedFile* and pass the file information through it. The parent component will receive this data through the *selectedFile* prop. In *ImageSelection*.jsx, add in **bold**:

```
...
function ImageSelection({selectedFile}) {
  const [selectedImage, setSelectedImage] = useState(null);

  const onFileSelected = (event) =>{
     const file = event.target.files[0];
     if (file) {
         const imageUrl = URL.createObjectURL(file);
         setSelectedImage(imageUrl);
         selectedFile(file);
     }
  }
  ...
```

Back in *dashboard/create-new/page*.jsx, let's create an *onHandleInputChange* method that accepts *value* and *fieldName* parameters. Add in **bold**:

```
function CreateNew() {

  const onHandleInputChange=(value,fieldName)=>{

  }

  return (
      <div>
          <h2 style={{
          ...
          }}>
              Create AI Interior
          </h2>
          <div className="grid grid-cols-2 gap-8 p-6">
            <div>
                <ImageSelection
                    selectedFile={(value) =>
                        onHandleInputChange(value,'image')}
                />
            </div>
...
```

And in *ImageSelection*, we'll call this method with the file value and 'image' as the field name. We will revisit and understand better how it works.

Adding a Form Section

Let's add a form section containing several components:
- Room type component
- Design/interior type component
- Additional specifications (optional text area) component
- and Generate image button

The whole thing will look something like:

Create AI Interior

Select Image of your room

[CHOOSE FILE] No file chosen

Select Room Type

[Select Room Type ▼]

Select Interior Design Type

Modern Industrial Bohemian Traditional

Rustic Minimalist

Enter Additional Requirements (Optional)

[Generate]

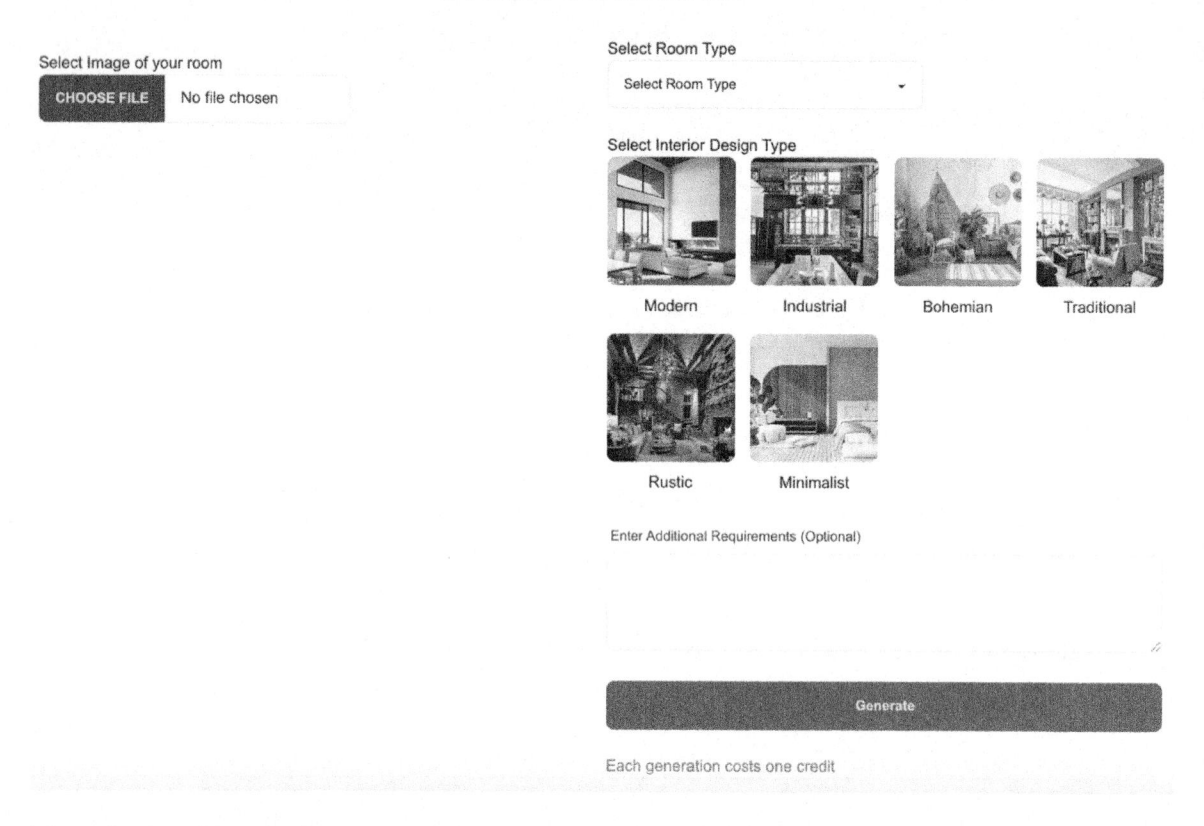

Each generation costs one credit

These fields will handle the user input for our interior design generation:

In *dashboard/create-new/_components*, let's create a component for room type called *RoomType*.jsx with a default template:

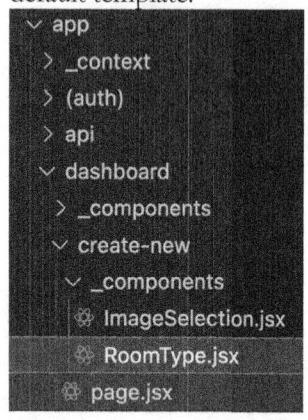

```
∨ app
  > _context
  > (auth)
  > api
  ∨ dashboard
    > _components
    ∨ create-new
      ∨ _components
          ImageSelection.jsx
          RoomType.jsx
          page.jsx
```

Then we'll import this *RoomType* component into .../ *create-new/page*.jsx file. In ...*dashboard/create-new/page*.jsx, add in **bold**:

...
import RoomType from './_components/RoomType'

```
function CreateNew() {
    ...
  return (
            ...
            <div className="grid grid-cols-2 gap-8 p-6">
               <div>
                  <ImageSelection
                     selectedFile={(value) =>
                        onHandleInputChange(value,'image')}
                  />
               </div>
```
               <div>
                  <RoomType />
               </div>
            ...

Back in *RoomType*.jsx, we use a *Select* component from DaisyUI (*daisyui.com/components/select/*):

Add in the below codes:

```
import React from 'react'

function RoomType() {
  return (
    <div>
        <label>Select Room Type</label>
        <div>
            <select
                className="select select-bordered w-full max-w-xs"
                required
```

```
                    defaultValue="" // Set default value to empty string
        >
                    <option value="" disabled>Select Room Type</option>
                    <option value="Living Room">Living Room</option>
                    <option value="Bedroom">Bedroom</option>
                    <option value="Kitchen">Kitchen</option>
                    <option value="Office">Office</option>
                    <option value="Bathroom">Bathroom</option>
            </select>
        </div>
    </div>
  )
}

export default RoomType
```

Code Explanation

```
    <div>
        <label>Select Room Type</label>
        <div>
            <select
                ...
                className="select select-bordered w-full max-w-xs"
                required
                defaultValue="" // Set default value to empty string
            >
                <option value="" disabled>Select Room Type</option>
                <option value="Living Room">Living Room</option>
                <option value="Bedroom">Bedroom</option>
                    ...
            </select>
        </div>
    </div>
```

We add a label "Select Room Type" and add the below room types as options:
- Living Room
- Bedroom
- Kitchen
- Office
- Bathroom

We set the initial option value to "Select Room Type" and disable it to make it mandatory for a user to select a drop down value:

Create AI Interior

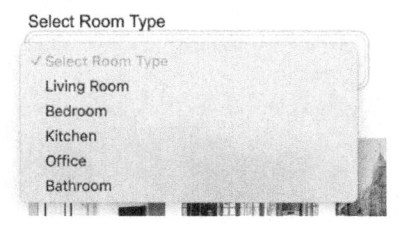

Next, we add an *onChange* method to the Select component that will capture the user's selection. Add in **bold**:

```
...
function RoomType({selectedRoomType}) {
  return (

    <div>
        <label>Select Room Type</label>
        <div>
            <select
                onChange={(e) => selectedRoomType(e.target.value)}
                className="select select-bordered w-full max-w-xs"
                required
                defaultValue="">
```

We'll pass this selected value through the *selectedRoomType* prop back to the parent component. Back in /dashboard/create-new/page.jsx, add the below in **bold**:

```
function CreateNew() {
    ...
  return (
            ...
            <div className="grid grid-cols-2 gap-8 p-6">
                <div>
                    <ImageSelection
                        ...
                    />
                </div>
                <div>
                    <RoomType
                        selectedRoomType={(value)=>
                            onHandleInputChange(value,'roomType')}
                    />
                </div>
                ...
```

We have *selectedRoomType* as a prop and use *onInputHandleChange* with 'roomType' as the field name and the selected value as the value parameter.

DesignType

Let's create a new component for the design type. We'll add a file in .../*create-new/components/* called *DesignType*.jsx:

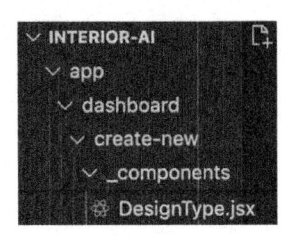

```
∨ INTERIOR-AI
  ∨ app
    ∨ dashboard
      ∨ create-new
        ∨ _components
          ⚙ DesignType.jsx
```

Add a default template to *DesignType*.jsx, save it, and import *DesignType* in .../*create-new/page*.jsx:

```
...
import RoomType from './_components/RoomType'
import DesignType from './_components/DesignType'

function CreateNew() {
    ...
    return (
        ...
        <div className="grid grid-cols-2 gap-8 p-6">
            ...
            <div>
                <RoomType
                    selectedRoomType={(value)=>
                        onHandleInputChange(value,'roomType')}
                />
                <DesignType />
            </div>
            ...
```

In .../*create-new/_components/DesignType*.jsx, let's add a *designs* array with different design styles.

```jsx
import React from 'react'

function DesignType() {
    const designs = [
        {
          name: 'Modern',
          image: '/modern.jpg',
        },
        {
          name: 'Industrial',
          image: '/industrial.jpg',
        },
        {
          name: 'Bohemian',
          image: '/bohemian.jpg',
        },
        {
          name: 'Traditional',
          image: '/traditional.jpg',
        },
        {
          name: 'Rustic',
          image: '/rustic.jpg',
        }, {
          name: 'Minimalist',
          image: '/minimalist.jpg',
        }
    ]

  return (
    <div>
        <label>Select Interior Design Type</label>
    </div>
  )
}
export default DesignType
```

The first one will be 'modern' with its corresponding image path. I've included some images (available in the source code – contact support@i-ducate.com) for different styles like modern, minimalistic, and industrial. So, make sure you have these images in your *public* folder:

```
∨ public
   bohemian.jpg
   industrial.jpg
   minimalist.jpg
   modern.jpg
   rustic.jpg
   traditional.jpg
```

Then we'll map through our *designs* array in .../*create-new*/*_components*/*DesignType*.jsx, by adding in **bold**:

```
function DesignType() {
  const designs = [
      ...
  ]

  return (
    <div>
        <label>Select Interior Design Type</label>
        <div className="grid grid-cols-4 gap-4">
            {designs.map((design, index) => (
                <div key={index}>
                    <img src={design.image} />
                    <h2 className="text-center mt-2 font-medium">
                      {design.name}
                    </h2>
                </div>
            ))}
        </div>
    </div>
  )
}
export default DesignType
```

Code Explanation

We also arrange the images in a grid format with `className="grid grid-cols-4 gap-4"`. This creates a row with 4 equally-sized and equally-spaced grid items.

```
<h2 className="text-center mt-2 font-medium">
    {design.name}
</h2>
```

Below each image, we display the design name using *design.name*. Now we can see all the different styles: Bohemian, Industrial, and the others.

Handling Hovering Effects

To handle hovering effects, add in **bold**:
```
function DesignType() {
    ...
    ...
        <div className="grid grid-cols-4 gap-4">
            {designs.map((design, index) => (
                <div key={index} className="cursor-pointer hover:opacity-80 transition-opacity">
                    <img src={design.image} />
                    <h2 className="text-center mt-2 font-medium">
                      {design.name}
                    </h2>
        ...
```

Whenever you hover over any image, it becomes slight transparent with a smooth transition animation and shows a pointer cursor to indicate it's clickable.

State Management

Now, when you select any of these design types, we need to save that selection in state. So add in **bold** below:
```
import React,{ useState } from 'react'

function DesignType() {
  const designs = [
      ...
  ]

  const [selectedOption, setSelectedOption] = useState();

  return (
    <div>
        <label>Select Interior Design Type</label>
        <div className="grid grid-cols-4 gap-4">
            {designs.map((design, index) => (
                <div key={index}
                  onClick={()=>{
                    setSelectedOption(design.name)
                  }}
                  className="cursor-pointer hover:opacity-80 transit...">
                    <img src={design.image} />
                    <h2 className="text-center mt-2 font-medium">
                      {design.name}
                    </h2>
                </div>
```

We create a *selectedOption* state variable.

In each design element, we'll add an *onClick* event. Here we set the *selectedOption* as the design name (*design.name*) since we want to track the active selection.

Showing Which Option Selected

For showing which option is click-selected, we add a border around the selected item. Add in the codes in **bold** below:

```
<div className="grid grid-cols-4 gap-4">
    {designs.map((design, index) => (
        <div key={index}
          onClick={()=>{
            setSelectedOption(design.name)
          }}
          className="cursor-pointer hover:opacity-80 … ">
            <div className={`aspect-square w-full
              relative overflow-hidden rounded-lg
              ${selectedOption === design.name ?
                'ring-4 ring-blue-500' : ''}`}>
                <img src={design.image} className="absolute inset-0
                  w-full h-full object-cover rounded-lg" />
            </div>
            <h2 className="text-center mt-2 font-medium">
                {design.name}
            </h2>
        </div>
    ))}
</div>
…
```

Code Explanation

We add a blue ring to the selected design image if *design.name* matches the *selectedOption*:

${selectedOption === design.name ? 'ring-4 ring-blue-500' : ''}

Let's see how it looks. When I select an item, you can see the border being added.

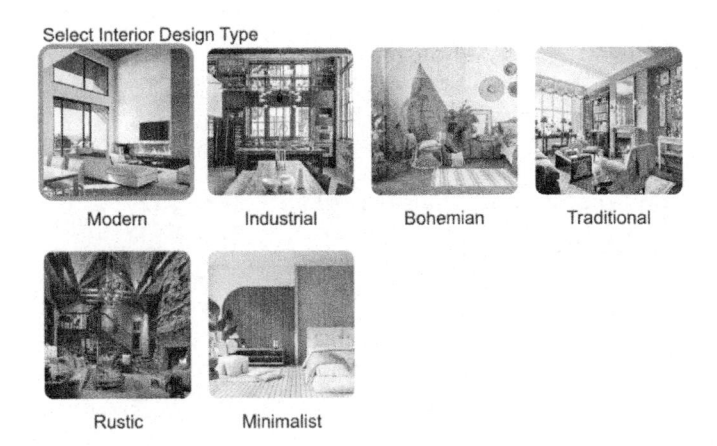

Now when you select anything, you can see the selection clearly.

But we still need to pass this selection up to the parent component. Add in **bold**:

```
function DesignType({selectedDesignType}) {
    ...

  return (
    <div>
        <label>Select Interior Design Type</label>
        <div className="grid grid-cols-4 gap-4">
            {designs.map((design, index) => (
                <div key={index}
                    onClick={()=>{
                        setSelectedOption(design.name);
                        selectedDesignType(design.name)
                    }}
                    ...
```

In the *onClick*, we make another call to `selectedDesignType` and pass *design.name*. We'll pass *selectedDesignType* up to the parent component in *../dashboard/create-new/page*.jsx. Add in **bold**:

../dashboard/create-new/page.jsx
...

```
function CreateNew() {
    ...
  return (
          ...
            <div>
```

```
        <RoomType
            selectedRoomType={(value)=>
                onHandleInputChange(value,'roomType')}
        />
        <DesignType
            selectedDesignType={(value)=>
                onHandleInputChange(value,'designType')}
        />
    </div>
    ...
```

Inside the parent component where we render *DesignType*, we call *onHandleInputChange*, passing both the value and the field name ("designType").

Text Area for Additional Prompts

Next, let's add a text area where users can enter additional requirements or specific prompts. This will let users input any extra details they want to include.

In *dashboard/create-new/_components/*, create a new component called *AdditionalReq*.jsx:

Inside the *AdditionalReq* component, we're going to add a text area. Let's look up the textarea component from DaisyUI:

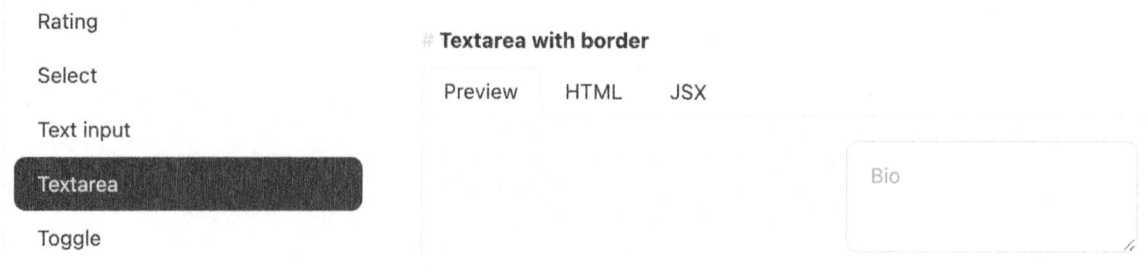

Fill in the codes:

```
import React from 'react'

function AdditionalReq() {
  return (
```

```
        <div>
            <div className="label">
                <span className="label-text">
                    Enter Additional Requirements (Optional)
                </span>
            </div>
            <textarea className="textarea textarea-bordered"></textarea>
        </div>
    )
}

export default AdditionalReq
```

To capture the user entered value and pass it back to the parent component, add the following:

```
function AdditionalReq({additionalReqInput}) {
    return (
        <div>
            ...
            ...
            <textarea className="textarea textarea-bordered h-24 w-full"
                onChange={(e) => additionalReqInput (e.target.value)}>
            </textarea>
        </div>
    )
}
```

We add an *onChange* method that takes an event parameter *(e)*. We create a prop *additionalReqInput* and pass the input through it back to the parent component.

Back in *../dashboard/create-new/page*.jsx, add in the below codes:

```
...
import AdditionalReq from './_components/AdditionalReq'

function CreateNew() {
    ...
    return (
            ...
            <div>
                <RoomType
                    selectedRoomType={(value)=>
                        onHandleInputChange(value,'roomType')}
                />
                <DesignType
```

```
                selectedDesignType={(value)=>
                    onHandleInputChange(value,'designType')}
            />
            <AdditionalReq
                additionalReqInput={(value)=>
                  onHandleInputChange(value,'additionalReqInput')}
            />
        </div>
    ...
```

We pass value and *additionalReqInput* as the field name to *onHandleInputChange*.

Generate Image Button

For the last component, we'll add a button to generate the image. Add in **bold**:

```
function CreateNew() {
    ...
  return (
            ...
        <div>
            <RoomType
                selectedRoomType={(value)=>
                    onHandleInputChange(value,'roomType')}
            />
            <DesignType
                selectedDesignType={(value)=>
                    onHandleInputChange(value,'designType')}
            />
            <AdditionalReq
                additionalReqInput={(value)=>
                  onHandleInputChange(value,'additionalReqInput')}
            />
            <button className="btn btn-primary w-full">
                Generate
            </button>
            <p className="text-gray-500">
                Each generation costs one credit
            </p>
        </div>
    ...
```

We add a button with the text "Generate". We style it with *w-full* for full width. We will implement the *onClick* of the button in the next chapter.

We also have a note below the button tag saying "`Each generation costs one credit`". See how cool and beautiful this page is looking right now:

Create AI Interior

Select Image of your room

CHOOSE FILE No file chosen

Select Room Type

Select Room Type ▾

Select Interior Design Type

Modern   Industrial   Bohemian   Traditional

Rustic   Minimalist

Enter Additional Requirements (Optional)

Generate

Each generation costs one credit

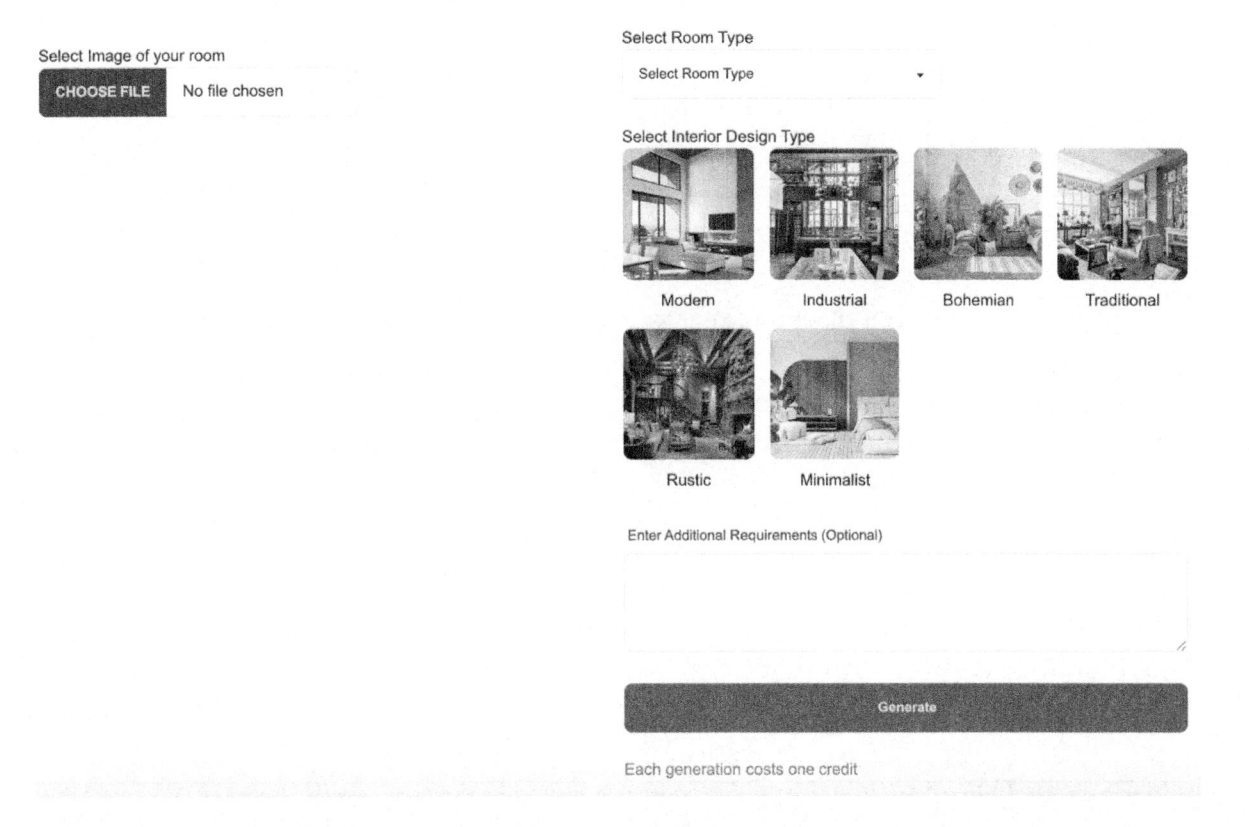

Saving All Values in One State

Now we want to save all these values in one state. When *Generate* is clicked, we'll make an API call to the AI model with these values. But first, we need to handle the values and field names we're passing to *onHandleInputChange* in */dashboard/create-new/page*.jsx. Add in **bold**:

/dashboard/create-new/page.jsx

```
import React, {useState} from 'react'
...
...

function CreateNew() {

  const [formData, setFormData] = useState([]);

  const onHandleInputChange=(value,fieldName)=>{
        setFormData(prevData => ({
            ...prevData,
            [fieldName]: value
        }));

        console.log(formData)
  }
  ...
  return (...)
```

Code Explanation

```
  const [formData, setFormData] = useState([]);
```

We define a *formData* state.

```
  const onHandleInputChange=(value,fieldName)=>{
        setFormData(prevData => ({
            ...prevData,
            [fieldName]: value
        }));

        console.log(formData)
  }
```

We update *formData* by using the previous state value and assign the new value to the corresponding field name.

To see the data, we *console.log(formData)* to check what's being saved.

Running our App

If you go back and refresh the page, then open the inspect panel's console, you'll see the data updating. When you select a room type (let's say "bedroom") and then select a design type, you'll see the values in the *formData* state type being logged in the console:

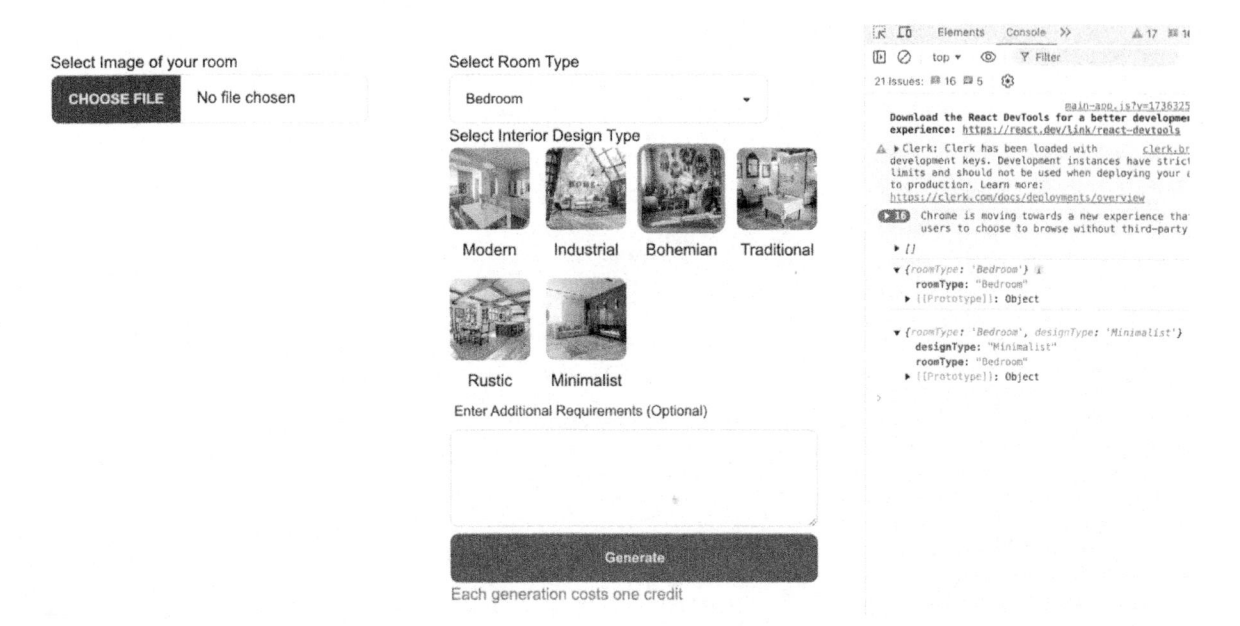

So that's how you can design this page to be simple and clean, while saving all selections in one state.

Next, we'll take all of these user selections and pass them to the AI image generator.

Chapter 7: Generate Interior Design with AI

Now we'll generate an AI image based on the uploaded image and selected options.

When the user clicks the "Generate" button, we'll first save the image to Firebase Storage. We will get back a URL for that image.

We then take the Firebase Storage URL and pass it to our AI API from Replicate, which will convert our uploaded image and return an AI redesigned version through a Replicate URL. Note that the URL from Replicate is only valid for 30-40 minutes.

Because of this time limitation, we need to convert that image to base64 format first, and then save it permanently in Firebase Storage

We then save the Firebase Storage AI image URL in our Neon PostgreSQL database using Drizzle.

That's an overview of the complete process flow. Things will get concrete as we proceed on.

Setup Firebase

Let's first set up Firebase to store our images. Go to firebase.google.com. If you don't have an account, create one - Firebase is free to use and provides 5GB of free storage, plus it's very easy to integrate.

Click on 'Go to console':

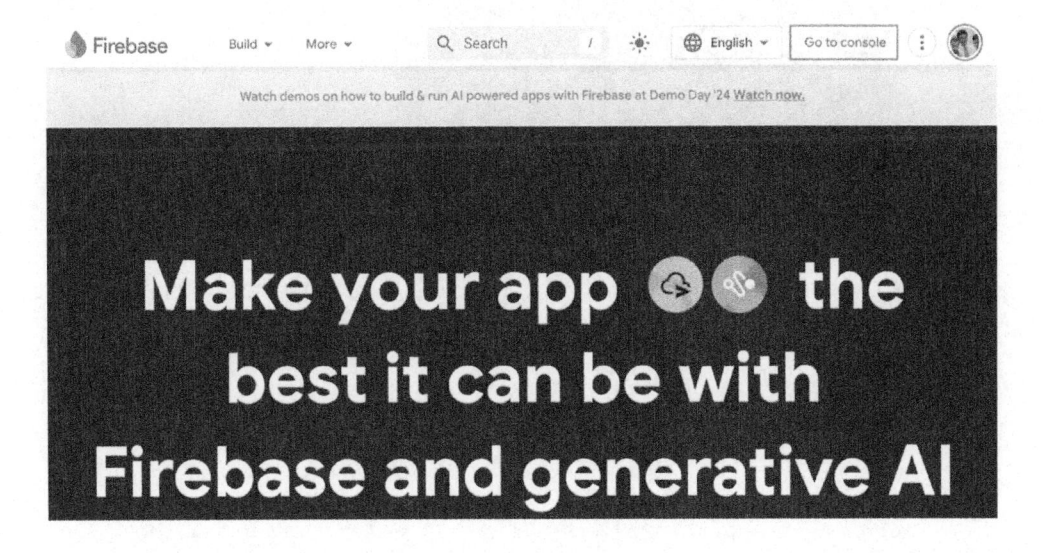

If you don't have a project yet, create a new one.

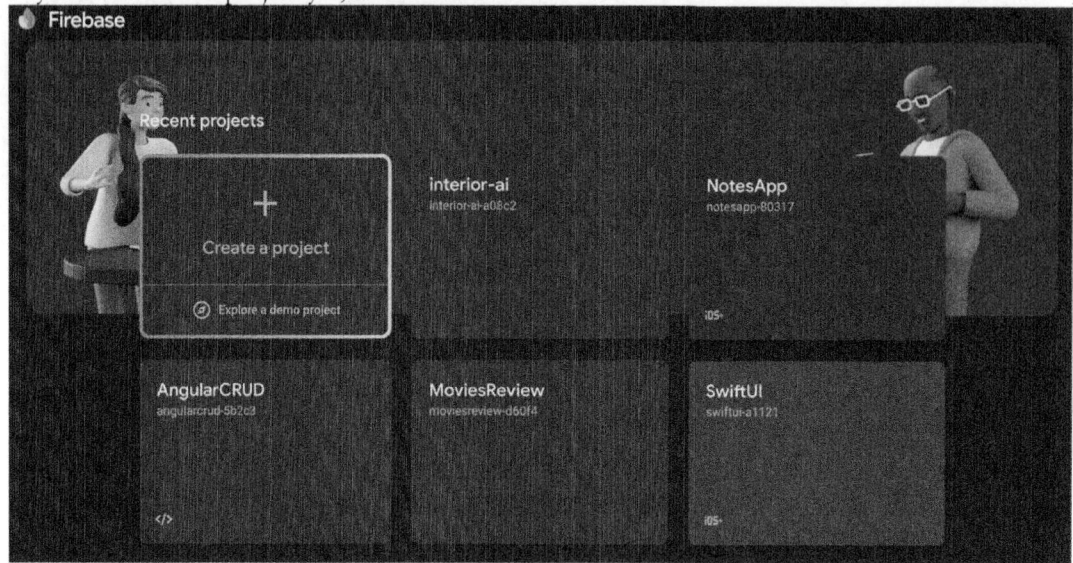

Enable the 'Storage' option in your Firebase project:

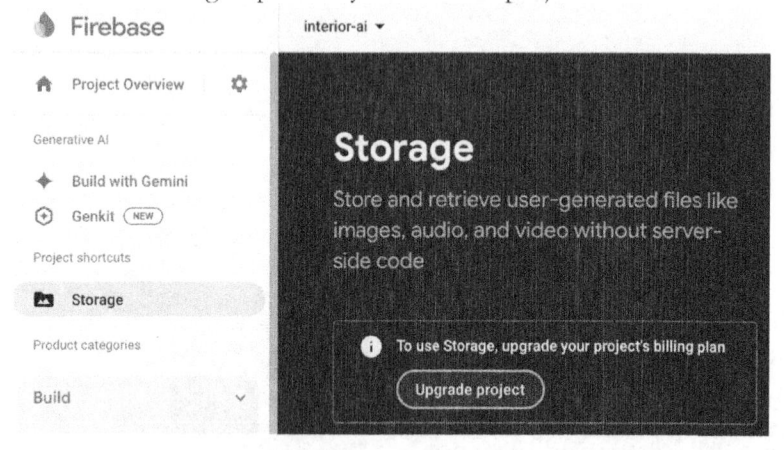

Note: you might have to 'Upgrade project' to use Storage. For e.g., I had to upgrade to the 'Blaze' plan which is 'pay as you go'.

After you have enabled Storage, go to your 'Project Overview' and click on 'web' as shown below:

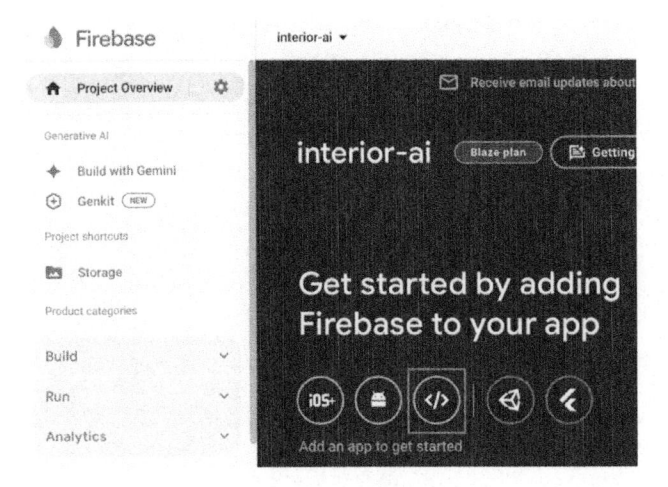

Here you need to give your application a name. I call mine "interior-ai":

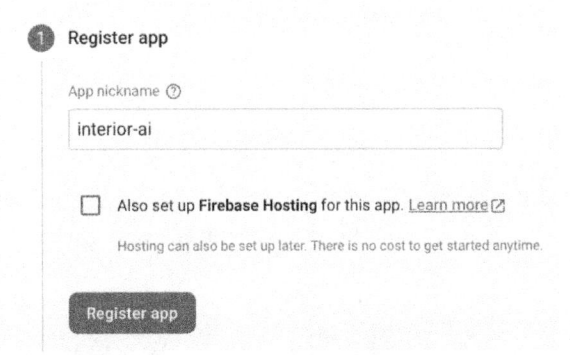

Register the application, and we'll get the configuration file:

Add Firebase SDK

```
// Import the functions you need from the SDKs you need
import { initializeApp } from "firebase/app";
// TODO: Add SDKs for Firebase products that you want to use
// https://firebase.google.com/docs/web/setup#available-libraries

// Your web app's Firebase configuration
const firebaseConfig = {
  apiKey: "AIzaSyB-FdBTn5t8xuab39ps-eQA-lEXvuKxpaU",
  authDomain: "interior-ai-a7641.firebaseapp.com",
  projectId: "interior-ai-a7641",
  storageBucket: "interior-ai-a7641.firebasestorage.app",
  messagingSenderId: "729374312025",
  appId: "1:729374312025:web:d057517c4ac9348ca05348"
};

// Initialize Firebase
const app = initializeApp(firebaseConfig);
```

First, we need to install Firebase. Go to the Terminal and paste the Firebase installation command:

```
npm install firebase
```

After installing Firebase in your application, you'll need to copy all of the config code from the documentation. Inside your *config* folder, create a new file called *firebaseConfig*.js:

```
INTERIOR-AI
> .next
> app
∨ config
  > .next
  JS db.js
  JS firebaseConfig.js
  JS schema.js
```

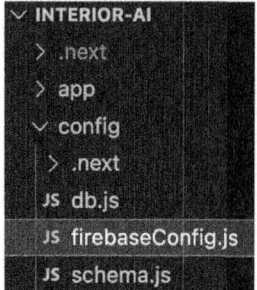

Paste the copied config code from the Firebase site into *firebaseConfig*.js (example):

```
import { initializeApp } from "firebase/app";

const firebaseConfig = {
  apiKey: "AIzaSyB-FdBTn5t8xuab39ps-eQA-aaaaa",
  authDomain: "interior-ai-a0000.firebaseapp.com",
  projectId: "interior-ai-a9999",
  storageBucket: "interior-ai-a7641.firebasestorage.app",
  messagingSenderId: "729374312025",
  appId: "1:729374312025:web:d057517c4ac9348ca05348"
};

const app = initializeApp(firebaseConfig);
```

Make sure you replace the above with your own config code.

Then, we'll export a storage reference by adding:

```
import { initializeApp } from "firebase/app";
import { getStorage } from "firebase/storage";

const firebaseConfig = {
    ...
    ...
};

const app = initializeApp(firebaseConfig);
export const storage = getStorage(app);
```

We can then use *storage* throughout the application.

Storage

Now, let's go to the Firebase console and navigate to *Storage* (you will be asked a serious of questions, just reply with the default options). Inside *Storage*, we'll create a new folder called "interior-ai".

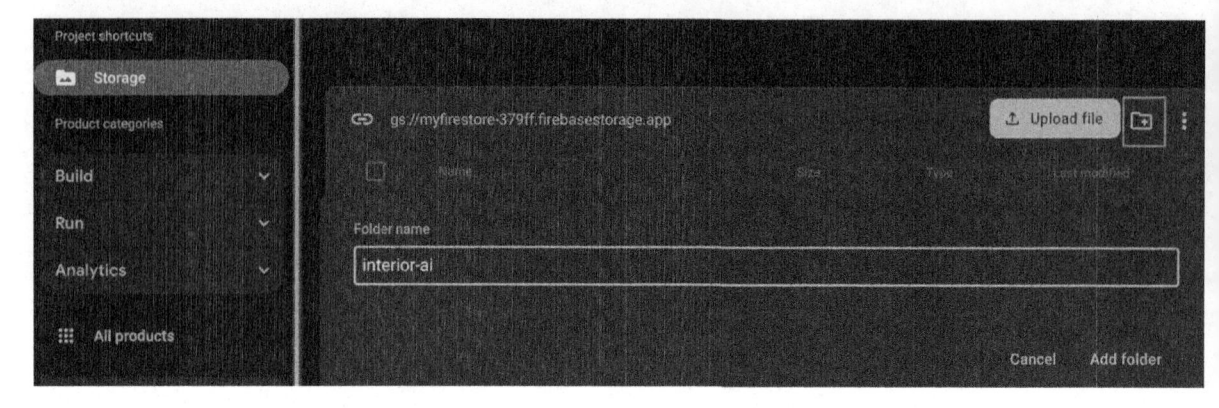

Once you create the folder, you'll see it in your storage. You can upload files manually here, but we want to use the Firebase SDK to handle uploads programmatically from code.

Setting Up Image Generation API

Now, let's get back to setting up the image generation and processing. We'll create a new API similar to the *verify-user* endpoint. Go to the *api* folder and create a new folder called "interior-ai". Inside *interior-ai*, create a new file *route*.jsx:

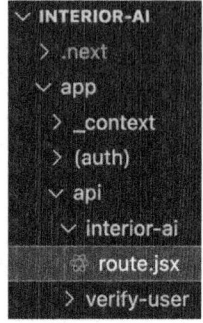

In it, let's create an async function for the POST request that takes a request parameter with the below code:

```
import { NextResponse } from "next/server";

export async function POST(request) {
    return NextResponse.json({
        result: "hello"
    });
}
```

We return a *NextResponse* with a simple JSON result that says "hello".

In *dashboard/create-new/page.jsx*, create a new method called *generateAIImage*. Add the below **codes**:

```
...
...
import axios from 'axios'

function CreateNew() {

    ...

    const onHandleInputChange=(value,fieldName)=>{
        setFormData(prevData => ({
            ...prevData,
            [fieldName]: value
        }));
    }

    const generateAIImage = async () => {

    }

    return (
        ...
            <RoomType .../>
            <DesignType .../>
            <AdditionalReq .../>
            <button onClick={generateAIImage} ...>Generate</button>
            <p className="...">Each generation costs one credit</p>
        ...
```

We' add the *onClick* handler for the 'Generate' button to call the *generateAIImage* method.

Inside *generateAIImage*, we'll make an API call using *axios*:

```
const generateAIImage = async () => {
    const result = await axios.post('/api/interior-ai', formData);
    console.log("result",result);
}
```

Here we make a POST request to */api/interior-ai* endpoint and pass *formData* in the request body. We can pass *formData* directly since it contains everything we need e.g. the room type, design type, uploaded image. These data elements will be included in the POST request to the API. After we get the result, let's *console.log(result)* to see what we're getting back.

Let's try to run our app. First, we'll upload an image and select a room type. Let's select "bedroom" as the room type, upload an image, and click 'Generate':

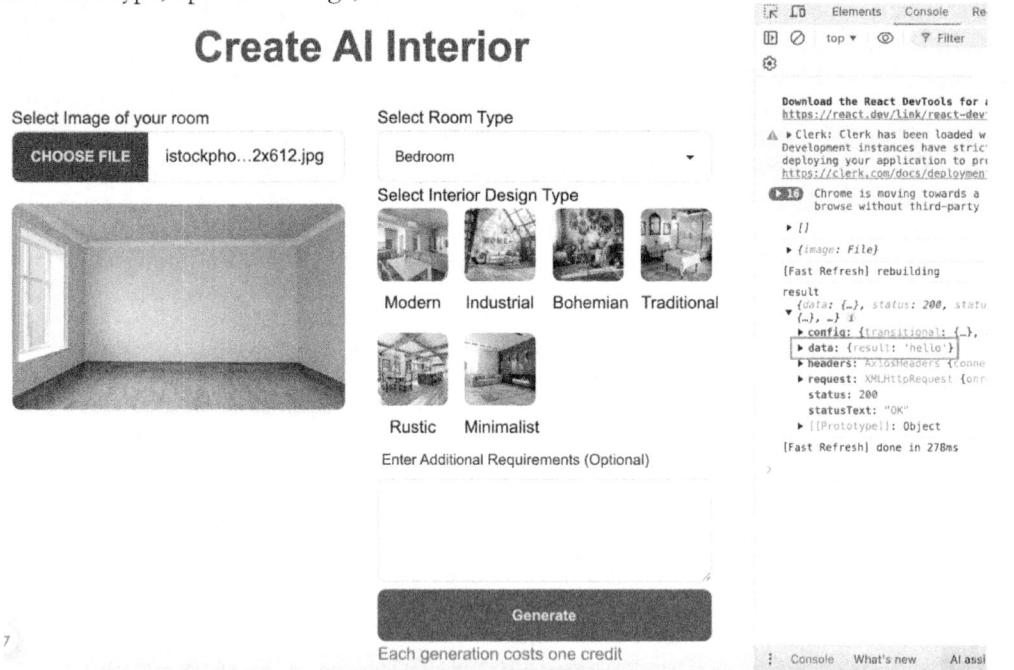

When we do this, you'll see the response in the console, with the data showing "result: hello" - confirming our API endpoint is working.

Saving our Image to Firebase

Now before making the API call, we need to save our image to Firebase. In ../*create-new/page*.jsx, let's create a new method called *saveRawImageToFirebase*. Add the codes:

...
...
```
import { ref, uploadBytes, getDownloadURL } from 'firebase/storage'
import { storage } from '../../../config/firebaseConfig'

function CreateNew() {
...

    const onHandleInputChange=(value,fieldName)=>{
       ...
    }

    const generateAIImage = async () => {
       ...
    }
```

```
        const saveRawImageToFirebase = async () => {
            const fileName = `${Date.now()}_raw.png`;
            const imageRef = ref(storage, `interior-ai/${fileName}`);

            await uploadBytes(imageRef,formData.image).then(resp=>{
                console.log('File Uploaded...')
            })

            const downloadUrl=await getDownloadURL(imageRef);
            console.log(downloadUrl);
            return downloadUrl;
        }
return (
...
```

Code Explanation

```
        const saveRawImageToFirebase = async () => {
            const fileName = `${Date.now()}_raw.png`;
```

We import *ref* from *firebase/storage* and create a unique filename using timestamp *Date.now()* and append '_raw.png'.

```
            const imageRef = ref(storage, `interior-ai/${fileName}`);
```

We then get the image reference using *ref* from Firebase storage, and the *storage* reference from our Firebase config. We specify the Firebase folder name ("interior-ai") followed by the filename.

```
            await uploadBytes(imageRef,formData.image).then(resp=>{
                console.log('File Uploaded...')
            })
```

Next, we upload the image reference along with the file. We use await *uploadBytes* and pass both the image reference and the file, which we'll get from *formData.image*.

To verify if the upload was successful, we add a console log that says 'file uploaded'.

```
            const downloadUrl=await getDownloadURL(imageRef);
```

After the file is uploaded, we get the URL of the uploaded image using *await getDownloadURL* from Firebase Storage. We pass the image reference to *getDownloadURL* to retrieve the download URL for that specific image and console log to verify in the console whether we successfully obtained the URL:

```
            console.log(downloadUrl);
            return downloadUrl;
```

That's how you can upload images to Firebase.

You might notice we're not showing any loading state right now, so users can't tell if it's actually uploading or not. We will implement that loading functionality later.

Testing our App

Let's now call *saveRawImageToFirebase* from our *generateAIImage* function. Add:

```
const generateAIImage = async () => {
    const rawImageUrl=await saveRawImageToFirebase();
    const result = await axios.post('/api/redesign-room', formData);
    console.log("result",result);
}
```

Before we can upload our image, to allow uploading of files to Firebase storage, back in the firebase storage console, under 'Rules':

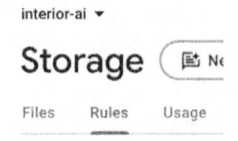

We give access to uploading and reading of files by having the below rules:

```
rules_version = '2';

service firebase.storage {
  match /b/{bucket}/o {
    match /{allPaths=**} {
      allow read, write: if true;  // This allows public access
    }
  }
}
```

Now go to our application to test it whether we received the image URL. Try uploading an image, select the room type, design type, and click 'Generate'.

In the console, you should see 'file uploaded' and the URL:

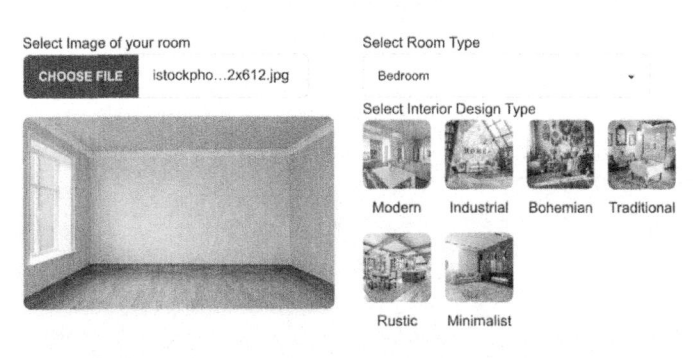

If you open the URL, you should see it:

The URL is fetched from Firebase Storage, and is the URL of the picture we just uploaded.

Calling 'interior-ai' API

After getting the URL, we need to pass it to the *interior-ai* API call we implemented earlier. In *../create-new/page*.jsx, add the below:

```
const generateAIImage = async () => {
    const rawImageUrl=await saveRawImageToFirebase();

    const result = await axios.post('/api/interior-ai', {
        imageUrl:rawImageUrl,
        roomType:formData?.roomType,
        designType:formData?.designType,
        additionalReq:formData?.additionalReq,
    })
    console.log("result",result);
}
```

We pass in the raw image URL, room type, design type and additional requirements from the form data. Now that we pass this information to the route, we need to retrieve it next.

In *../api/interior-ai/route.jsx*, we'll destructure the request data by add:

```
export async function POST(request) {

    const {imageUrl, roomType, designType, additionalReq} = await request.json()

    return NextResponse.json({
        result: "hello"
    });
}
```

This is how we can destructure all the fields from whatever you passed in the request body.

Convert Image using AI

The next step is to convert the image using AI. We're going to use Replicate, which is a comprehensive source of AI APIs. First, if you don't have an account, create a free one at replicate.com. Click on "Get Started":

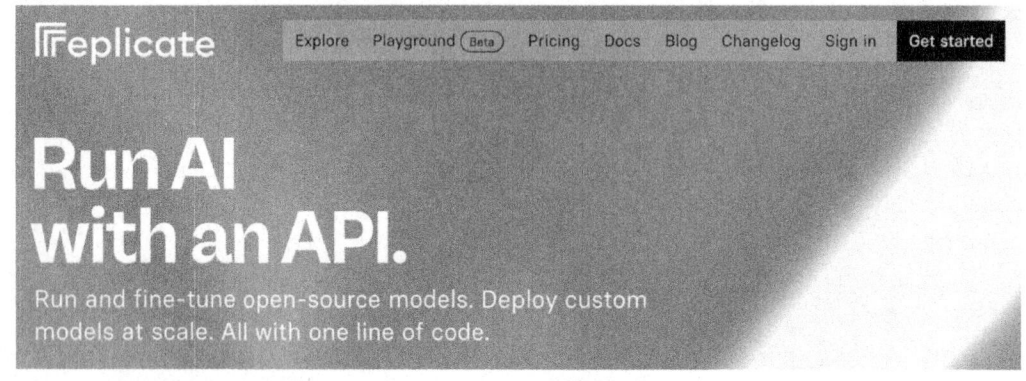

Go to 'Account Settings':

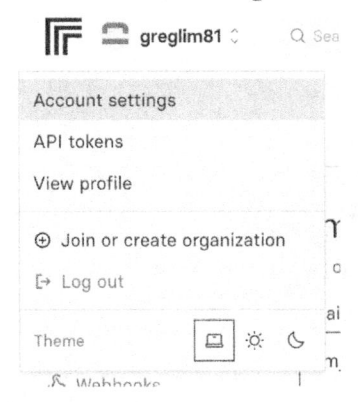

You'll need to add your billing information under 'Billing':

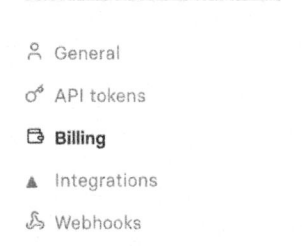

You'll also need to create an API token under 'API tokens':

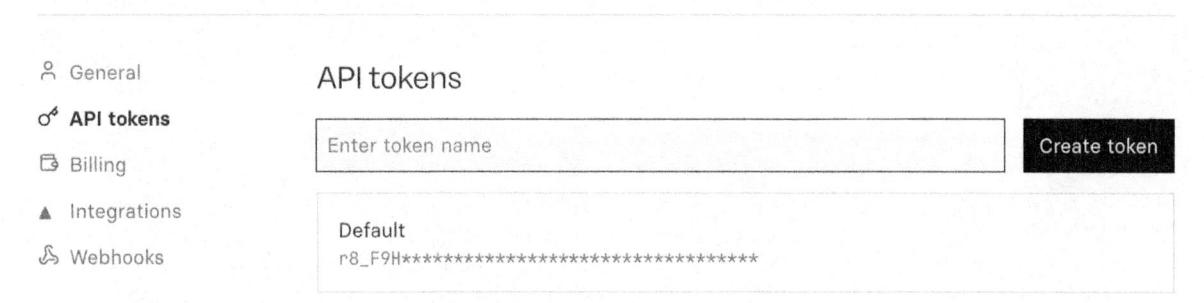

Click on "Explore" and you'll find various AI models to choose from:

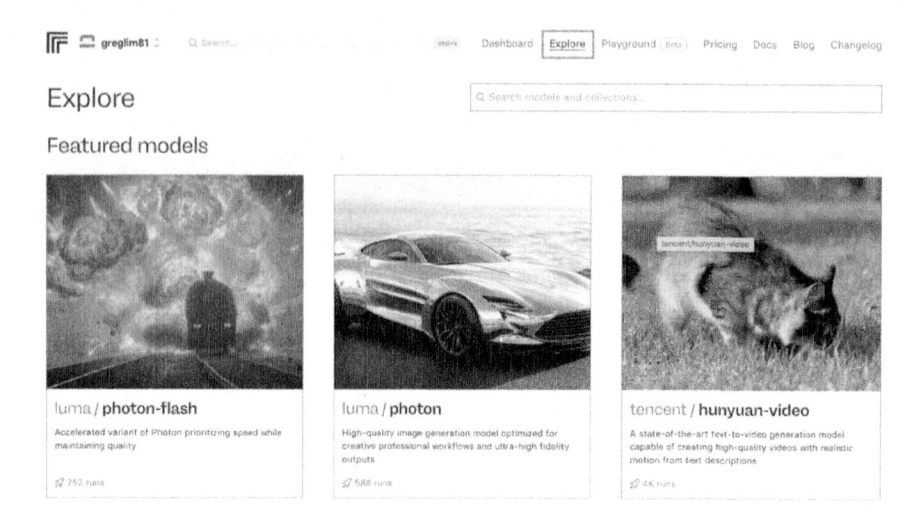

To find the model we need, let's search for "interior design":

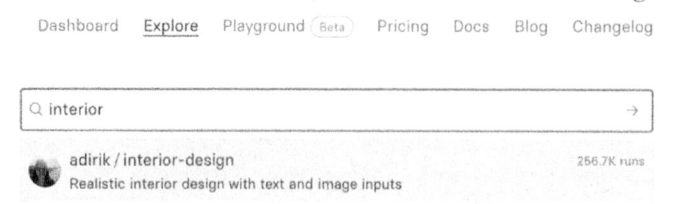

This is the specific model we'll be using. Provide an input, and it will generate a beautiful output for you:

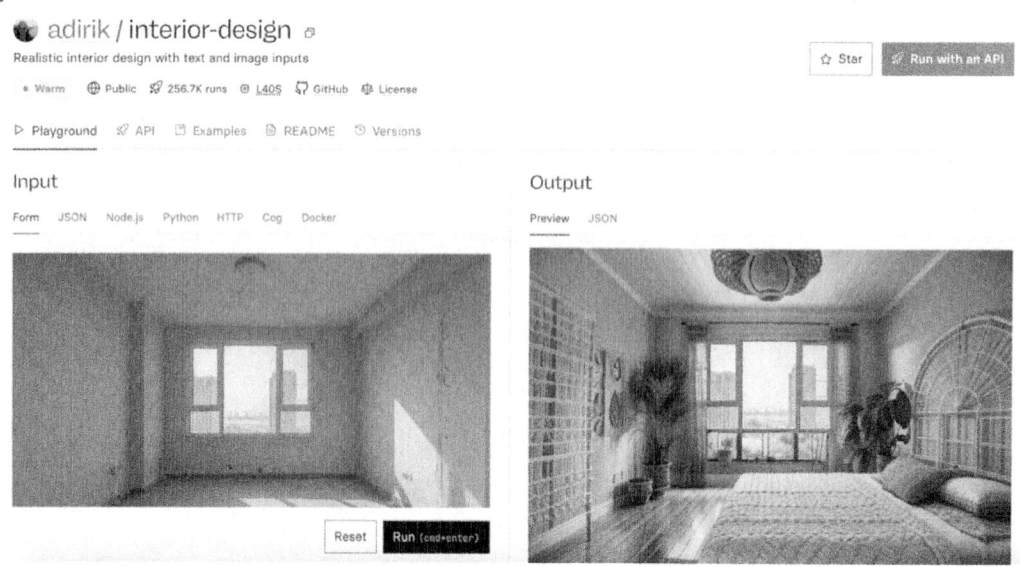

You can also include a prompt:

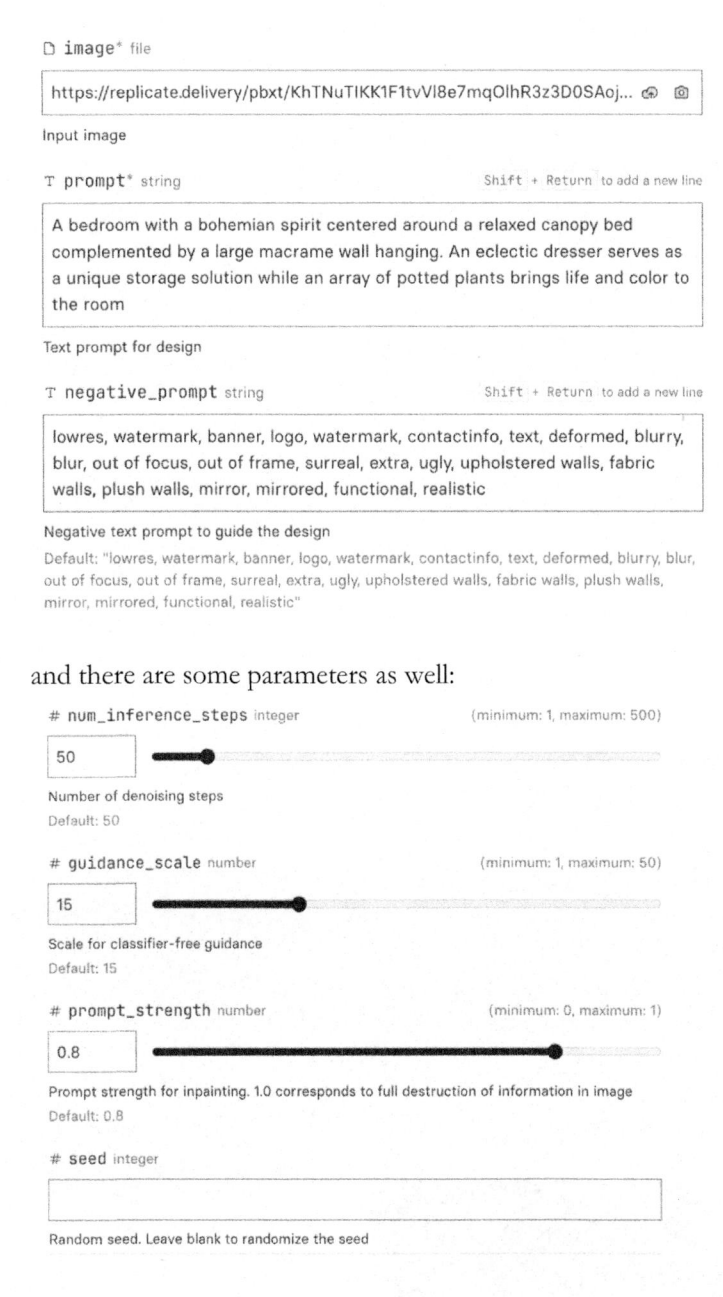

image* file

`https://replicate.delivery/pbxt/KhTNuTIKK1F1tvVl8e7mqOlhR3z3D0SAoj...`

Input image

prompt* string   Shift + Return to add a new line

> A bedroom with a bohemian spirit centered around a relaxed canopy bed complemented by a large macrame wall hanging. An eclectic dresser serves as a unique storage solution while an array of potted plants brings life and color to the room

Text prompt for design

negative_prompt string   Shift + Return to add a new line

> lowres, watermark, banner, logo, watermark, contactinfo, text, deformed, blurry, blur, out of focus, out of frame, surreal, extra, ugly, upholstered walls, fabric walls, plush walls, mirror, mirrored, functional, realistic

Negative text prompt to guide the design
Default: "lowres, watermark, banner, logo, watermark, contactinfo, text, deformed, blurry, blur, out of focus, out of frame, surreal, extra, ugly, upholstered walls, fabric walls, plush walls, mirror, mirrored, functional, realistic"

and there are some parameters as well:

num_inference_steps integer   (minimum: 1, maximum: 500)

`50`

Number of denoising steps
Default: 50

guidance_scale number   (minimum: 1, maximum: 50)

`15`

Scale for classifier-free guidance
Default: 15

prompt_strength number   (minimum: 0, maximum: 1)

`0.8`

Prompt strength for inpainting. 1.0 corresponds to full destruction of information in image
Default: 0.8

seed integer

Random seed. Leave blank to randomize the seed

For this particular model's cost, you can generate up to 185 images for just one dollar, which is quite

Run time and cost

This model costs approximately $0.0054 to run on Replicate, or 185 runs per $1, but this varies depending on your inputs. It is also open source and you can run it on your own computer with Docker.

To see how much you've spent, go to your dashboard.

This model runs on Nvidia L40S GPU hardware. Predictions typically complete within 6 seconds.

Note: So don't worry about incurring huge API costs while going through this book. It will probably just cost a few cents.

Keep in mind that different models in Replicate have different price tags.

Now, to use this model, let's go to the API section and select Node.js:

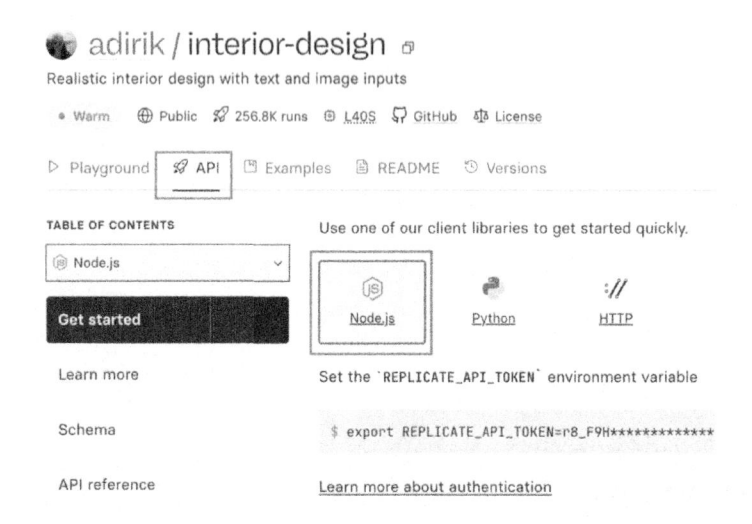

adirik / interior-design

Realistic interior design with text and image inputs

- Warm   ⊕ Public   ⚡ 256.8K runs   ⊕ L40S   ⚙ GitHub   ⚖ License

▷ Playground   ⚡ API   📖 Examples   📄 README   🕘 Versions

TABLE OF CONTENTS

Node.js

Get started

Learn more

Schema

API reference

Use one of our client libraries to get started quickly.

Node.js   Python   HTTP

Set the `REPLICATE_API_TOKEN` environment variable

$ export REPLICATE_API_TOKEN=r8_F9H**************

Learn more about authentication

Next, we copy the Replicate API Key:

Set the `REPLICATE_API_TOKEN` environment variable

$ export REPLICATE_API_TOKEN=r8_F9H************************************ and specify it in our *.env* file (remember to add 'NEXT_PUBLIC'):

```
...
...
NEXT_PUBLIC_CLERK_SIGN_IN_URL=/sign-in
NEXT_PUBLIC_CLERK_SIGN_UP_URL=/sign-up
NEXT_PUBLIC_REPLICATE_API_TOKEN=r8_F9Hq...
```

Install and Import Replicate

Next, install the Replicate SDK by running:

```
npm install replicate
```

Once it's installed, import Replicate by adding in *…/api/interior-ai/route*.jsx:

```
import { NextResponse } from "next/server";
import Replicate from "replicate";

const replicate = new Replicate({
    auth: process.env.NEXT_PUBLIC_REPLICATE_API_TOKEN
});

export async function POST(request) {

    const {imageUrl, roomType, designType, additionalReq} = await request.json()

    return NextResponse.json({
        result: "hello"
    });

}
```

Our Replicate instance is now ready to use. We next need to define both the *input* and *output* sections:

```
Run adirik/interior-design using Replicate's API. Check out the model's schema for an overview of inputs and outputs.

import Replicate from "replicate";
const replicate = new Replicate();

const input = {
    image: "https://replicate.delivery/pbxt/KhTNuTIKK1F1tvVl8e7mqOlhR3z3DQSAojAMN8BNftCvAubM/bedroom_3.jpg",
    prompt: "A bedroom with a bohemian spirit centered around a relaxed canopy bed complemented by a large macrame wall 
};

const output = await replicate.run("adirik/interior-design:76604baddc85b1b4616e1c6475eca080da339c8875bd4996705440484a6ea
```

Copy these lines from the documentation and paste them in */api/interior-ai/route*.jsx:

```
...
const replicate = new Replicate({
    auth: process.env.NEXT_PUBLIC_REPLICATE_API_TOKEN
});

export async function POST(request) {

    const {imageUrl, roomType, designType, additionalReq} = await request.json()

    try{
      const input = {
        image: "https://replicate.delivery/pbxt/KhTNuT...
        /bedroom_3.jpg",
        prompt: "A bedroom with a bohemian spirit centered around a relaxed canopy bed complemented by a large macrame wall hanging..."
      };
      const output = await replicate.run("adirik/interior-design:766...38",
            { input });
    }
    catch(e){

    }

    return NextResponse.json({
        result: "hello"
    });
}
```

Note: we wrap them in a *try-catch* block to handle any exceptions.

Inside *output*, we call *replicate.run* with our model API name and version. These model details are essential for the API call.

Passing Parameters into Image Configuration

In the *input* configuration, let's pass our custom parameters for the prompt. Make the code changes below in **bold**:

```
...
export async function POST(request) {
    const { imageUrl, roomType, designType, additionalReq } = await request.json()

    try{
        const input = {
            image: imageUrl,
            prompt: 'A ' + roomType + " with a " + designType + " style interior " + additionalReq
        };
        const output = await replicate.run("adirik/interior-design:766...38",{ input });

        ...
```

For example, if we select "bedroom" as the room type and "modern" as the design type, our prompt will be "A bedroom with modern style interior". This is a simple, clean prompt, and you can include any additional requirements.

Returning the Output and Converting it to Base Image URL

When we have the output from the AI model, we need to first convert it to a base image URL so that we can store it in our Firebase storage.

To convert this output URL to base64, let's create a new async function called *ConvertImageToBase64* that accepts an *imageURL* parameter. In *.../api/interior-ai/route*.jsx, add in **bold**:

```
...
import axios from "axios";
...
...

    async function ConvertImageToBase64(imageUrl){
        const resp=await axios.get(imageUrl,{responseType:'arraybuffer'});
        const base64ImageRaw=Buffer.from(resp.data).toString('base64');

        return "data:image/png;base64,"+base64ImageRaw;
    }
```

Code Explanation

```
        const resp=await 
axios.get(imageUrl,{responseType:'arraybuffer'});
```

We use *axios.get* with *imageURL* and set the response type as 'arraybuffer' which tells axios to return the raw binary data as an *ArrayBuffer* instead of parsing it as JSON or text.

```
        const base64ImageRaw=Buffer.from(resp.data).toString('base64');
```

We take the binary data (*resp.data*) and create a *Buffer* from it. We convert the buffer to a base64 string encoding. Base64 encoding represents binary data using a set of 64 ASCII characters, making it safe to transmit in text-based protocols

```
        return "data:image/png;base64,"+base64ImageRaw;
```

We create a Data URL by combining the prefix *data:image/png;base64*, which tells browsers "this is base64-encoded PNG image data".

Call `ConvertImageToBase64`

Let's call `ConvertImageToBase64` by adding the below:

```
import { storage } from '../../../config/firebaseConfig'
import { getDownloadURL, ref, uploadString } from "firebase/storage";
...
...

export async function POST(request) {
     ...
    try{
        const input = {
            image: imageUrl,
            prompt: 'A ' + roomType + " with a " + designType + " style interior " + additionalReq
        };

        const output = await replicate.run("adirik/interior-design:766...38",{ input });

        const base64Image=await ConvertImageToBase64(output);

        const fileName=Date.now()+'.png';
        const storageRef=ref(storage,'interior-ai/'+fileName);
```

```
        await uploadString(storageRef,base64Image,'data_url');
        const downloadUrl=await getDownloadURL(storageRef);
        console.log(downloadUrl);
        return NextResponse.json({'result':downloadUrl});
    }
    catch(e){
        return NextResponse.json({
            error: e
        });
    }
```

Code Explanation

```
        const base64Image=await ConvertImageToBase64(output);
```

We create a *base64Image* constant that awaits our *ConvertImageToBase64* function, passing in our URL as the parameter.

```
        const fileName=Date.now()+'.png';
```

Create a filename using *Date.now()* with a *.png* extension.

```
        const storageRef=ref(storage,'interior-ai/'+fileName);
```

We set up a storage reference.

```
        await uploadString(storageRef,base64Image,'data_url');
```

Next, use *await uploadString* since we're uploading a base64 image, not bytes. Pass in *storageRef*, *base64Image*, and set the type as 'data_url'.

```
        const downloadUrl=await getDownloadURL(storageRef);
        console.log(downloadUrl);
        return NextResponse.json({'result':downloadUrl});
```

Now we'll get the *downloadURL* and log *downloadURL* to the console and return it in our response.

Testing our App

Let's save these changes and in our app, click 'Generate'. The URL should be saved and we can see it in the server console:

```
 GET /dashboard/create-new 200 in 41ms
downloadUrl: https://firebasestorage.googleapis.com/v0/b/interior-ai-a7641.fireb
asestorage.app/o/interior-ai%2F1736474163586.png?alt=media&token=6dd303c8-99cc-4
62b-a030-de334d24d15e
 POST /api/interior-ai 200 in 9680ms
```

You can also see it in the browser console:

If we copy the URL and paste it in the browser, we should see the image now saved on Firebase:

If we go to the Firebase console, we can see several saved images, including our latest one:

After saving the image as base64 and storing it in Firebase, our final step is to save everything to the database.

Saving to the Database

Let's implement database storage by first creating a new table 'aiGeneratedImage' in our database. In /config/schema.js, add:

```
import { pgTable } from 'drizzle-orm/pg-core'
import { serial, varchar, integer } from 'drizzle-orm/pg-core'

export const Users = pgTable('users', {
  id: serial('id').primaryKey(),
  name: varchar('name').notNull(),
  email: varchar('email').notNull(),
  imageUrl: varchar('image_url').notNull(),
  credits: integer('credits').default(3)
});

export const AiGeneratedImage = pgTable('aiGeneratedImage', {
  id: serial('id').primaryKey(),
  roomType: varchar('roomType').notNull(),
  designType: varchar('designType').notNull(),
  orgImage: varchar('orgImage').notNull(),
  aiImage: varchar('aiImage').notNull(),
  userEmail: varchar('userEmail')
})
```

And in the Terminal, run:

```
npx drizzle-kit push
```

This updates the schema. After the changes are applied, stop and run drizzle-kit studio again:

```
npx drizzle-kit studio
```

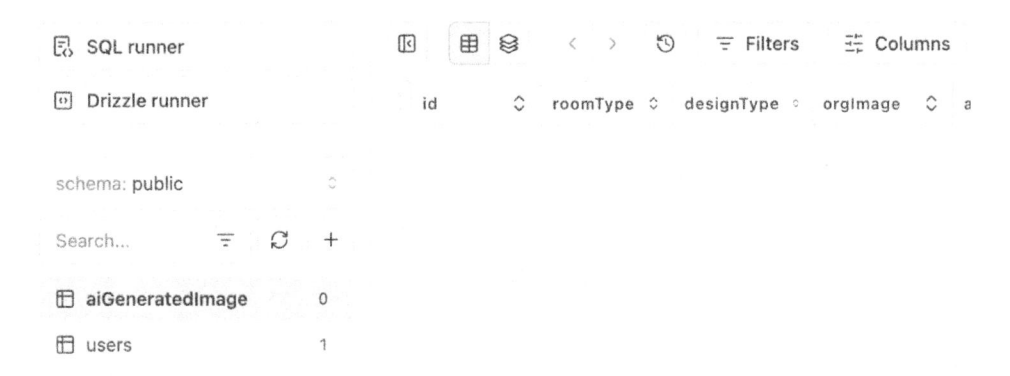

In Drizzle Kit Studio, we should see our new table called 'aiGeneratedImage'.

In our */api/interior-ai/route*.jsx, let's add the database insert. Add the below:

```
...
...
import { db } from "../../../config/db";
import { AiGeneratedImage } from "../../../config/schema";

export async function POST(request) {
    ...
    try{
        const input = {
            image: imageUrl,
            prompt: ...
        };

        ...
        const storageRef=ref(storage,'interior-ai/'+fileName);
        await uploadString(storageRef,base64Image,'data_url');
        const downloadUrl=await getDownloadURL(storageRef);
        console.log(downloadUrl);
```

```
        const dbResult=await db.insert(AiGeneratedImage).values({
            roomType:roomType,
            designType:designType,
            orgImage:imageUrl,
            aiImage:downloadUrl,
            userEmail:userEmail
        }).returning({id:AiGeneratedImage.id});

        console.log(dbResult);
        return NextResponse.json({'result': downloadUrl});
    }
    catch(e){
        return NextResponse.json({
            error: e
        });
    }
}
```

For the insert statement, we specify `returning({id:AiGeneratedImage.id})`. We also console.log `dbResult` to see what we receive.

But currently, we have not gotten `userEmail` yet. Let's get user information by adding in ../*create-new/page*.jsx:

```
..
..
import { useUser } from '@clerk/nextjs'

function CreateNew() {

    const {user}=useUser();
    const [formData, setFormData] = useState([]);
 ...
```

And then in *GenerateAiImage*:
```
    const generateAIImage = async () => {
        setLoading(true);
        const rawImageUrl=await saveRawImageToFirebase();

        const result = await axios.post('/api/interior-ai', {
            imageUrl:rawImageUrl,
            roomType:formData?.roomType,
            designType:formData?.designType,
            additionalReq:formData?.additionalReq,
            userEmail:user?.primaryEmailAddress?.emailAddress
        });
        ...
        ...
```

Back inside */api/interior-ai/route*.jsx, we'll destructure the user email from the request:

```
...
export async function POST(request) {
  const { imageUrl, roomType, designType, additionalReq, userEmail } =
      await request.json()
  ...
```

So that we can use it over here:

```
            const dbResult=await db.insert(AiGeneratedImage).values({
                roomType:roomType,
                designType:designType,
                orgImage:imageUrl,
                aiImage:downloadUrl,
                userEmail:userEmail
            }).returning({id:AiGeneratedImage.id});
```

Let's try running our app again: upload the image, select room type and interior design type, then click 'Generate'. Once generated, it should be saved to our database:

id	roomType	designType	orgImage	aiImage	userEmail
2	Kitchen	Modern	https://firebasestorage.g…	https://firebasestorage.googl…	limjunqu@gma…

In Drizzle Studio, we've got the email address along with both the original and AI-generated images URLs. That's how you can save the results to our database.

The next thing we need to do is add a loading indicator by the AI generation is going on. This will let users know when the system is making API calls in the background. Let's implement this in the next chapter.

Chapter 8: Custom Loading

When we click 'Generate', while waiting for the AI Image generation on the server-side, we'll show a loading indicator using a DaisyUI *Loading* component (*daisyui.com/components/loading/*):

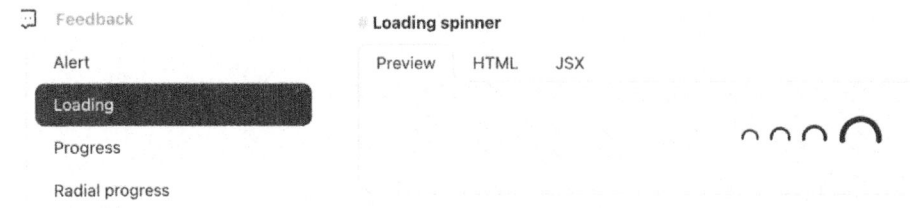

To house this loader, go to the *dashboard/create-new/_components* folder and create a new file called *CustomLoading*.jsx with the codes:

```
import React from 'react'

function CustomLoading() {
    return (
      <div>
          <span className="loading loading-spinner loading-lg"></span>
          <h2>Redesigning your room...do not refresh</h2>
      </div>
    )
}

export default CustomLoading
```

We'll display the loading indicator only when there's a server-side API call happening. For this, in */create-new/page*.jsx, we'll maintain a state called 'loading'. Add in **bold**:

...
import CustomLoading from './_components/CustomLoading'

function CreateNew() {

    const {user}=useUser();
    const [formData, setFormData] = useState([]);
    const [loading, setLoading] = useState(false);
    ...

We'll set its initial value to false. When the image starts generating, we'll set the *loading* state to true. Add in **bold**:

```
    const generateAIImage = async () => {
        setLoading(true);
        const rawImageUrl=await saveRawImageToFirebase();

        const result = await axios.post('/api/interior-ai', {
            ...
        });

        setLoading(false);
        console.log("result",result.data);
    }
        ...
```

When we get the generated result, we'll set *loading* back to false.

In *../create-new/page*.jsx, we'll render the custom loading indicator when *loading* is true, else - render the form as before. Add in **bold**:

```
function CreateNew() {
    ...
    ...
    return (
        <div>
            <h2 style={{
                ...
            }}>
                Create AI Interior
            </h2>

            {loading ? (
                <CustomLoading />
            ) : (
                <div className="grid grid-cols-2 gap-8 p--6">
                    <div className="p-4 ...">
                        <ImageSelection .../>
                    </div>
                    <div className="rounded-lg ...">
                        <RoomType .../>
                        <DesignType .../>
                        <AdditionalReq .../>
                        ...
                    </div>
                </div>
            )}
        </div>
    )
```

Let's save it and try generating an image. We have this loading animation showing on the screen:

Interior AI

Create AI Interior

⟳

Redesigning your room...do not refresh

When the image generation is complete, the loader will disappear. But we have yet to show the generated image. Let's do that in the next chapter.

Chapter 9: Display Output

Once the AI image is generated, we'll show a dialog displaying both the original image and the AI-generated image. You'll see a slider that you can move left to right to compare the original image with the AI-generated one:

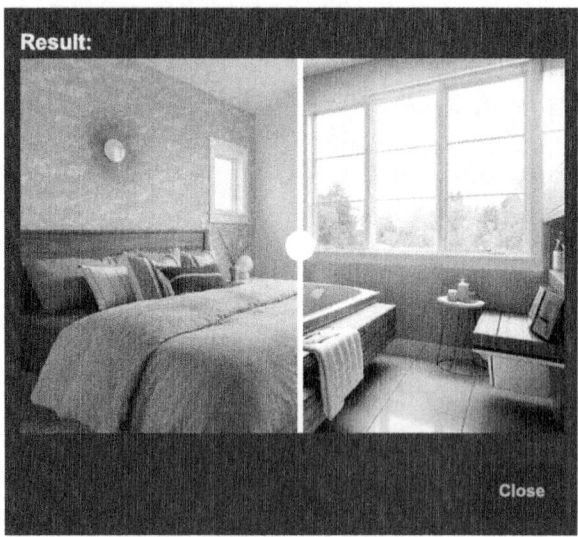

There's also a close button to dismiss the dialog.

For this, we'll use the *react-before-after-slider component* (github.com/smeleshkin/react-before-after-slider-component).

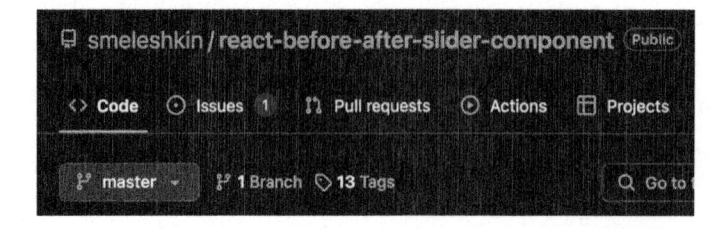

Looking at this example, you'll see the original image on the left and the AI-generated image on the right:

React before after slider component

Simple slider component for comparing images. Before and after.

So copy the *npm* command and run it in the Terminal:

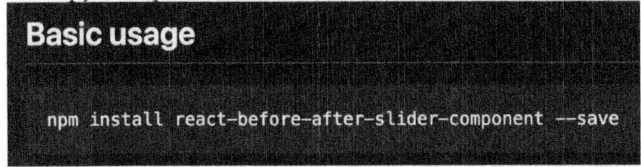

Basic usage

```
npm install react-before-after-slider-component --save
```

Now, let's go to */dashboard/create-new/page*.jsx. First, we'll create a state for the AI generated image. We'll add:

```
...
function CreateNew() {

    const {user}=useUser();
    const [formData, setFormData] = useState([]);
    const [loading, setLoading] = useState();
    const [aiOutputImage, setAiOutputImage] = useState();
...
```

When we get the result, we'll set the AI output image by adding:

```
    const generateAIImage = async () => {
        setLoading(true);
        const rawImageUrl=await saveRawImageToFirebase();

        const result = await axios.post('/api/interior-ai', {
```

```
        ...
        ...
    });

    setAiOutputImage(result.data.result)

    setLoading(false);
    console.log("result",result.data);
}
```

We'll use *setAiOutputImage* and set it to *result.data.result*, which contains the output image URL:

```
result
▼ {data: {…}, status: 200, s
  {…}, …} i
  ▶ config: {transitional: {.
  ▼ data:
    ▶ result: {id: 3}
    ▶ [[Prototype]]: Object
```

Next, we'll create a new state that represents if a dialog containing the slider component should appear. Add:

```
...
function CreateNew() {

    const {user}=useUser();
    const [formData, setFormData] = useSta       te([]);
    const [loading, setLoading] = useState();
    const [aiOutputImage, setAiOutputImage] = useState();
    const [openOutputDialog, setOpenOutputDialog] = useState(false);
    ...
```

We'll set its initial value to false, meaning don't show the dialog with the slider component yet.

Once the image output is generated, we'll set *openOutputDialog* to true to display it. Add:

```
    const generateAIImage = async () => {
        ...
        const result = await axios.post('/api/interior-ai', {
        ...
        });

        setAiOutputImage(result.data.result)
        setOpenOutputDialog(true);
        setLoading(false);
    }
```

Next, we'll have to create the *AiOutputDialog* component inside the *dashboard/create-new/_components* folder. Create a new file called *AiOutputDialog*.jsx:

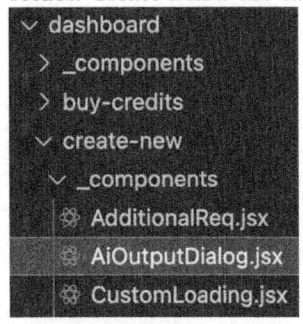

In *AiOutputDialog.jsx*, we will use the Modal component from DaisyUI:

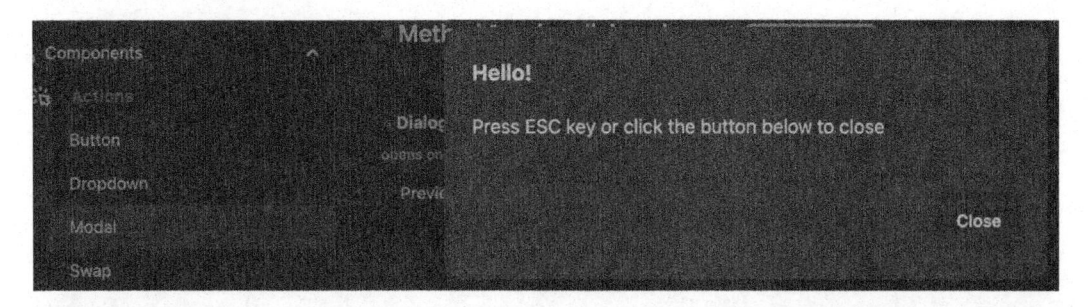

We will modify the example code a little:

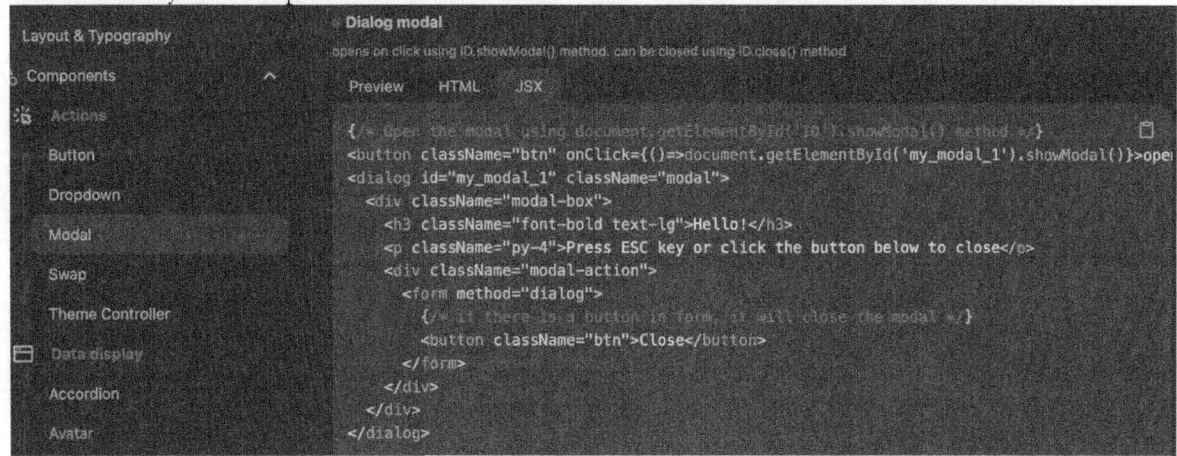

We don't need the button, so I'll remove it. We'll just show the dialog. Fill in *AiOutputDialog*.jsx with the below (you can get the source code from support@i-ducate.com):

```jsx
import React, {useEffect} from 'react'
import ReactBeforeSliderComponent from 'react-before-after-slider-component';
import 'react-before-after-slider-component/dist/build.css';

function AiOutputDialog({openDialog, setOpenDialog, orgImage,aiImage}) {
    useEffect(() => {
        if (openDialog) {
          document.getElementById('my_modal_1').showModal();
          }
        }
      , [openDialog]);

    const handleClose = () => {
        setOpenDialog(false);
    };

  return (
    <div>
        <dialog id="my_modal_1" className="modal">
            <div className="modal-box">
                <h3 className="font-bold text-lg">Result:</h3>
                <ReactBeforeSliderComponent
                    firstImage={{
                        imageUrl:aiImage
                    }}
                    secondImage={{
                        imageUrl:orgImage
                    }}
                />
                <div className="modal-action">
                    <form method="dialog">
                        <button className="btn" onClick={handleClose} >Close</button>
                    </form>
                </div>
            </div>
        </dialog>
    </div>
  )
}

export default AiOutputDialog
```

Code Explanation

```
import ReactBeforeSliderComponent from 'react-before-after-slider-
component';
import 'react-before-after-slider-component/dist/build.css';
```

Here we need to import `ReactBeforeSliderComponent` first. We copy the CSS along with the import for that component.

Back in the `ReactBeforeSliderComponent` component documentation, we can see that the first image is provided via an object that contains the image URL:

```
import React from 'react';
import ReactBeforeSliderComponent from 'react-before-after-slider-component';
import 'react-before-after-slider-component/dist/build.css';

const FIRST_IMAGE = {
  imageUrl: 'https://example.com/.../some-image.jpg'
};
const SECOND_IMAGE = {
  imageUrl: 'https://example.com/.../some-image-2.jpg'
};
/* ... */
<ReactBeforeSliderComponent
    firstImage={FIRST_IMAGE}
    secondImage={SECOND_IMAGE}
/>
/* ... */
```

So that's why we have:

```
function AiOutputDialog({openDialog, setOpenDialog, orgImage, aiImage}) {
     ...
  return (
    <div>
        ...
              <ReactBeforeSliderComponent
                  firstImage={{
                      imageUrl:aiImage
                  }}
                  secondImage={{
                      imageUrl:orgImage
                  }}
              />
```

We need to ensure that when passing the image URL, you pass it inside a field called *imageUrl*. We have the first image and second image to pass. We will talk about how to get *aiImage* and *orgImage* later.

```jsx
            <ReactBeforeSliderComponent
                firstImage={{
                    ...
                secondImage={{
                    ...
            />
            <div className="modal-action">
                <form method="dialog">
                    <button className="btn"
                            onClick={handleClose} >Close</button>
                </form>
            </div>
```

After that, we'll add a Close button. When the user clicks close, we'll set *openDialog* to false.

```
function AiOutputDialog({openDialog, setOpenDialog, orgImage,aiImage}) {
    useEffect(() => {
        if (openDialog) {
          document.getElementById('my_modal_1').showModal();
          }
        }
    , [openDialog]);

    const handleClose = () => {
        setOpenDialog(false);
    };
```

We'll pass the *openDialog* prop above. When the user clicks close, we'll set *openDialog* to false. *useEffect* detects if there's a change in value in *openDialog*, and if *openDialog* is true, show the modal.

Original Image and AI Image Props

Back in *../create-new/page*.jsx, we import and render the `AiOutputDialog` component in **bold**:

...
...
import AiOutputDialog from './_components/AiOutputDialog'

```
            ...
            {loading ? (
                <CustomLoading />
            ) : (
                <div className="grid grid-cols-2 gap-8 p-6">
                    ...
```

```
            <div className="rounded-lg shadow-sm space-y-6">
                <RoomType .../>
                <DesignType .../>
                <AdditionalReq .../>
                ...
                <p className="text-gray-500">
                    Each generation costs one credit
                </p>
            </div>
            <AiOutputDialog
                openDialog={openOutputDialog}
                setOpenDialog={setOpenOutputDialog}
                orgImage={orgImage}
                aiImage={aiOutputImage}
            />
        </div>
    )}
    ...
```

In rendering the *AIOutputDialog* component, we'll pass in *openDialog, setOpenDialog* state and two more props:
- *orgImage*
- *aiOutputImage*

We haven't yet create a state for the original image. So let's add:

```
function CreateNew() {

    const {user}=useUser();
    const [formData, setFormData] = useState([]);
    const [loading, setLoading] = useState();
    const [aiOutputImage, setAiOutputImage] = useState();
    const [openOutputDialog, setOpenOutputDialog] = useState(false);
    const [orgImage,setOrgImage]=useState();
    ...
```

And from when we save the original image to Firebase storage, we *setOrgImage*:

```
    const saveRawImageToFirebase = async () => {
        const fileName = `${Date.now()}_raw.png`;
        const imageRef = ref(storage, `interior-ai/${fileName}`);

        await uploadBytes(imageRef,formData.image).then(resp=>{
            console.log('File Uploaded...')
        })
```

```
        const downloadUrl=await getDownloadURL(imageRef);
        console.log(downloadUrl);
        setOrgImage(downloadUrl);
        return downloadUrl;
    }
```

With this, we now can pass *orgImage* and the *aiImage*, to the *AiOutputDialog* component:

```
<AiOutputDialog
                openDialog={openOutputDialog}
                setOpenDialog={setOpenOutputDialog}
                orgImage={orgImage}
                aiImage={aiOutputImage}
/>
```

And that's why back in */create-new/_components/AiOutputDialog*, we can pass in *aiImage* for the first image, and *oriImage* for the second image:

```
function AiOutputDialog({openDialog, setOpenDialog, orgImage, aiImage}) {
    ...
    return (
      <div>
        ...
                <ReactBeforeSliderComponent
                    firstImage={{
                        imageUrl:aiImage
                    }}
                    secondImage={{
                        imageUrl:orgImage
                    }}
                />
```

Testing our App

Let's test this out. Upload an image, select the room type, style, and click 'Generate'. And you can see this beautiful modal where you can slide to compare the images:

On the left you have the original image and on the right you'll see the beautifully AI generated image. You can see all the elements in the original image remain in place (e.g. windows, doors remain in their exact locations), just redesigned according to the AI model. And when you click close, the modal disappears.

Our results are also saved in our database:

id	roomType	designType	orgImage	aiImage	userEmail
2	Kitchen	Modern	https://firebasestorage.g…	https://firebasestorage.googl…	limjunqu@gma…
3	Office	Industrial	https://firebasestorage.g…	https://firebasestorage.googl…	limjunqu@gma…
4	Kitchen	Modern	https://firebasestorage.g…	https://firebasestorage.googl…	limjunqu@gma…
5	Kitchen	Traditional	https://firebasestorage.g…	https://firebasestorage.googl…	limjunqu@gma…
6	Office	Industrial	https://firebasestorage.g…	https://firebasestorage.googl…	limjunqu@gma…
7	Kitchen	Bohemian	https://firebasestorage.g…	https://firebasestorage.googl…	limjunqu@gma…
8	Bathroom	Bohemian	https://firebasestorage.g…	https://firebasestorage.googl…	limjunqu@gma…

We have the details like the original image, AI image, room type, and user information.

This chapter shows how you can generate AI images and display them in a professional looking way. This *react-before-after-slider* helps us present a comparison between the old and new images.

Chapter 10: Display User's Images

Now we'll display all the rooms the user has created on their dashboard:

Let's return to our *dashboard/_components/Listing/page*.jsx file. Currently in *Listing*, when a user doesn't have any rooms generated yet, we show the "`No Interior AI Designs Generated Yet`" message:

```
function Listing() {
  ...
  return (
    <div>
        ...
        {userRoomList?.length == 0 ?
            <div className="..." >
                No Interior AI Designs Generated Yet
            </div>
            :
            <div>

            </div>
        }
    </div>
  )
}
```

Let's create a new function *GetUserRoomList* in the *Listing* component by adding in **bold**:

...
...
```
import { db } from '../../../config/db';
import { desc, eq } from 'drizzle-orm';
import { AiGeneratedImage } from '../../../config/schema';

function Listing() {

    const {user} = useUser();
      ...
      ...
    const GetUserRoomList=async()=>{
        const result=await db.select().from(AiGeneratedImage)
        .where(eq(AiGeneratedImage.userEmail,
            user?.primaryEmailAddress?.emailAddress))
        .orderBy(desc( AiGeneratedImage.id))

        console.log(result);
    }
  ...
```

GetUserRoomList get the user's AI generated images from the database based on the user's email address

We make it async since we're awaiting the database query and log the result to see what we get.

`GetUserRoomList` needs to be called within *useEffect* and triggered when the user information is available. Add in **bold**:

```
...
import React, {useState, useEffect} from 'react'

function Listing() {
    ...
    useEffect(()=>{
        user&&GetUserRoomList();
    },[user])

   const GetUserRoomList=async()=>{
       ...
```

Let's now test our app. Go to the dashboard and check the console, and we've got some records:

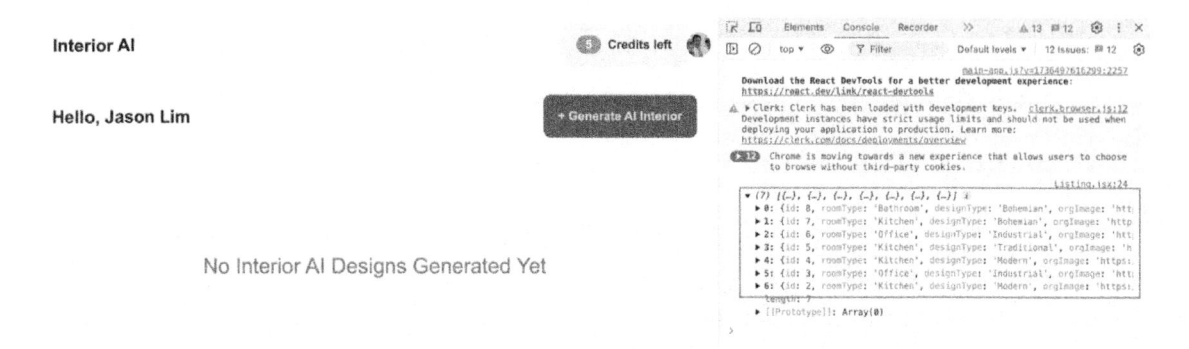

Let's save these records in a *userRoomList* state:

```
function Listing() {

    const {user} = useUser();
    const [userRoomList, setUserRoomList] = useState([]);
    ...

    const GetUserRoomList=async()=>{
        const result=await db.select().from(AiGeneratedImage)
        .where(eq(AiGeneratedImage.userEmail,user?.primaryEmailAddress?..

        setUserRoomList(result);
        console.log(result);
    }
```

Now when I save this and refresh the screen, you'll see we're not displaying "No Interior AI Designs Generated Yet" anymore because we have data. Since we have *userRoomList*, it will jump to this new block in **bold**:

```
        {userRoomList?.length == 0 ?
            <div className="flex justify-center items-center h-full text-
2xl text-gray-500 mt-32">
                No Interior AI Designs Generated Yet
            </div>
            :
            <div>
            ...{/* Listing */}
            </div>
        }
```

Let's now iterate through the Room List information. We'll map through *userRoomList* as shown in **bold**:

```
...
...
import RoomDesignCard from './RoomDesignCard';

function Listing() {
    ...
    ...

        {userRoomList?.length == 0 ?
            <div className="...">
                No Interior AI Designs Generated Yet
            </div>
            :
            <div>
                {userRoomList.map((room,index)=>(
                    <div key={index}>
                        <RoomDesignCard room={room}></RoomDesignCard>
                    </div>
                ))}
            </div>
    }
```

In */dashboard/_components/*, we will create a new component called *RoomDesignCard*.jsx which we use inside the *map*. Let's give *RoomDesignCard.jsx* a default template for now:

```
import React from 'react'

function RoomDesignCard() {
  return (
    <div>
      RoomDesignCard
    </div>
  )
}

export default RoomDesignCard
```

When you run the app now, you can see on the screen, we are rendering the text "RoomDesignCard":

Interior AI   5 Credits left

Hello, Jason Lim   + Generate AI Interior

RoomDesignCard
RoomDesignCard
RoomDesignCard
RoomDesignCard
RoomDesignCard
RoomDesignCard
RoomDesignCard

RoomDesignCard Component

Next, we'll pass each room's information to this Room Design card component. In *RoomDesignCard*.jsx, add in **bold**:

```
import React from 'react'
import ReactBeforeSliderComponent from 'react-before-after-slider-component';
import 'react-before-after-slider-component/dist/build.css';

function RoomDesignCard({room}) {

  return (
    <div>
        <ReactBeforeSliderComponent
            firstImage={{
                imageUrl:room?.aiImage,
            }}
            secondImage={{
                imageUrl:room?.orgImage,
            }}
        />
    </div>
  )
}
```

The `RoomDesignCard` component accepts a 'room' prop. We then proceed to use the `ReactBeforeSliderComponent` which we have used previously.

For the first image URL, we'll use *room?.aiImage*. For the second image URL, we'll use *room?.orgImage*. Make sure the names match the column names in the database table exactly i.e.: 'aiImage' and 'orgImage'.

Next, in *Listing*.jsx, add:

```
...
{userRoomList?.length == 0 ?
    <div className="...">
        No Interior AI Designs Generated Yet
    </div>
    :
    <div className="grid grid-cols-3 gap-4">
        {userRoomList.map((room,index)=>(
            <div key={index}>
                <RoomDesignCard room={room} />
            </div>
        ))
...
```

We add *className="grid grid-cols-3 gap-4"* to display the items in a grid format with three columns.

Below each image, we can add two more pieces of information.

142

- room's room type
- room's design type

Add in **bold**:
```
function RoomDesignCard({room}) {

  return (
    <div>
        <ReactBeforeSliderComponent
            ...
            ...
        />
        <div>
          <p>🏠 Room Type: {room.roomType}</p>
          <p>🎨 Design Type: {room.designType}</p>
        </div>
    </div>
  )
}
```

We also add emoji icons to these labels. Feel free to make any additional styling changes you'd like:

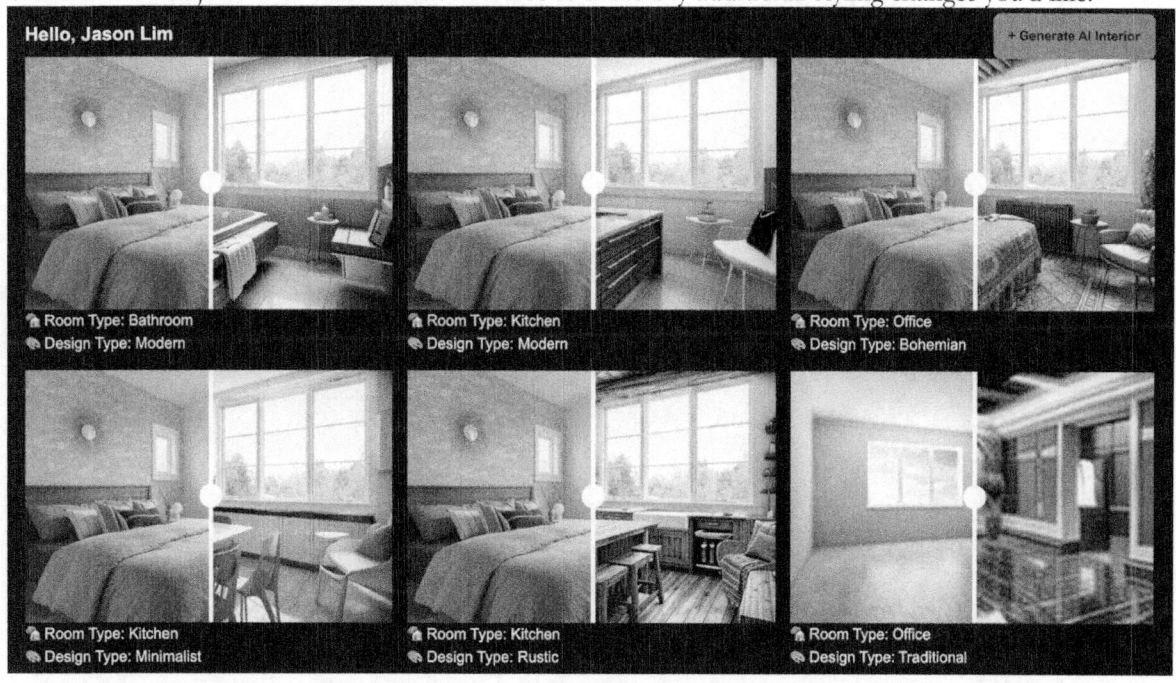

Currently, these cards aren't clickable, but let's do so by wrapping an *onClick* handler to each *RoomDesignCard* component in .../*dashboard*/*_components*/*Listing*.jsx:

```
...
const [openDialog,setOpenDialog]=useState(false);
const [selectedRoom,setSelectedRoom]=useState()
...
...
<div className="grid grid-cols-3 gap-4">
    {userRoomList.map((room,index)=>(
        <div key={index}
            onClick={()=>{setOpenDialog(true);setSelectedRoom(room)}}>
            <RoomDesignCard room={room}></RoomDesignCard>
        </div>
    ))}
</div>
```

When a user clicks on a room, it selects the current selected room and sets *openDialog* to true which render the *AiOutputDialog* component (similar to what we did earlier when we generated the image). Add in **bold**:

```
...
...
```
`import AiOutputDialog from '../create-new/_components/AiOutputDialog'`
```

function Listing() {
    ...
    return (
        <div>
            ...
            {userRoomList?.length == 0 ?
                <div className="...">
                    No Interior AI Designs Generated Yet
                </div>
                :
                <div className="grid grid-cols-3 gap-4">
                    {userRoomList.map((room,index)=>(
                    ...
                    ))}
                </div>
            }
```
`            <AiOutputDialog openDialog={openDialog}`
`                setOpenDialog={setOpenDialog}`
`                aiImage={selectedRoom?.aiImage}`
`                orgImage={selectedRoom?.orgImage}`
`            />`
```
        </div>
    )
}
```

We have used *AiOutputDialog* before. But to recap, it needs several props:
- *openDialog* state (set to true when a user clicks on a room)
- *setOpenDialog*
- *aiImage* from *selectedRoom?.aiImage*
- *orgImage* from *selectedRoom?.originalImage*

Now, when you click on an image, it will show *AIOutputDialog*.

Chapter 11: Payment Gateway

When users click 'Buy More Credits', they're given the option to purchase additional credits. We will create a new route *localhost:3000/dashboard/buy-credits* to handle the purchase process:

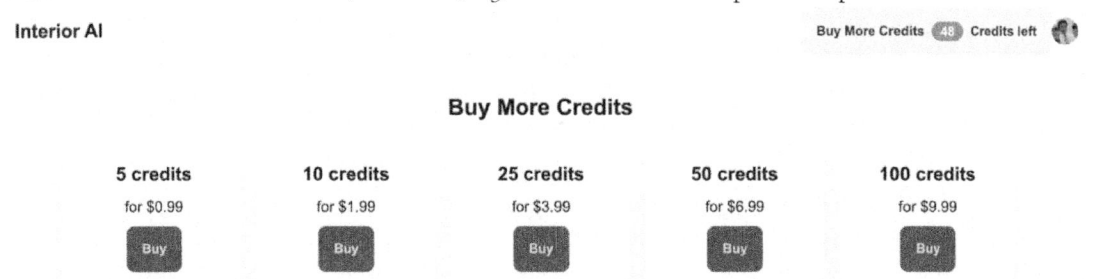

We will add different credit purchase options. Users can choose to buy anywhere from 5 to 100 credits, with pricing shown below each option.

In *dashboard*, create a new folder *buy-credits*, and in it, create *page*.jsx. Let's add different credit package options, each showing the number of credits and their corresponding price by adding the below codes:

```
"use client"
import React, {useState } from 'react'

function BuyCredits() {

    const [selectedOption,setSelectedOption]=useState([]);

    const creditsOption=[
        {
          credits:5,
          amount:0.99
        },
        {
          credits:10,
          amount:1.99
        },
        {
          credits:25,
          amount:3.99
        },
        {
          credits:50,
          amount:6.99
```

```
      },
      {
        credits:100,
        amount:9.99
      },
    ]

  return (
    <div>
        <div className="text-2xl font-bold text-center mb-6">
            Buy More Credits
        </div>
        <div className="flex flex-row gap-4 justify-center">
           {creditsOption.map((item,index)=>(
              <div key={index} className="card bg-base-100 w-48 shadow-xl">
                 <div className="card-body p-4 place-items-center">
                     <h2 className="card-title">
                          {item.credits} credits
                     </h2>
                     <p>for ${item.amount}</p>
                     <button className="btn btn-primary"
                           onClick={()=>setSelectedOption(item)}>
                           Buy
                     </button>
                 </div>
              </div>
           ))}
        </div>
    </div>
  )
}
export default BuyCredits
```

Note: you can get the source codes from support@i-ducate.com

Code Explanation

```
    const [selectedOption,setSelectedOption]=useState([]);
```

We have the *selectedOption* state which holds the selected option.

We then iterate through the *creditOptions* array to display the various credit purchase options:

```jsx
        {creditsOption.map((item,index)=>(
            <div key={index} className="card bg-base-100 w-48 shadow-xl">
                <div className="card-body p-4 place-items-center">
                    <h2 className="card-title">
                        {item.credits} credits
                    </h2>
                    <p>for ${item.amount}</p>
                    <button className="btn btn-primary"
                        onClick={()=>setSelectedOption(item)}>
                        Buy
                    </button>
                </div>
            </div>
        ))}
```

We display each credit purchase option in a DaisyUI Card component (*daisyui.com/components/card/*):

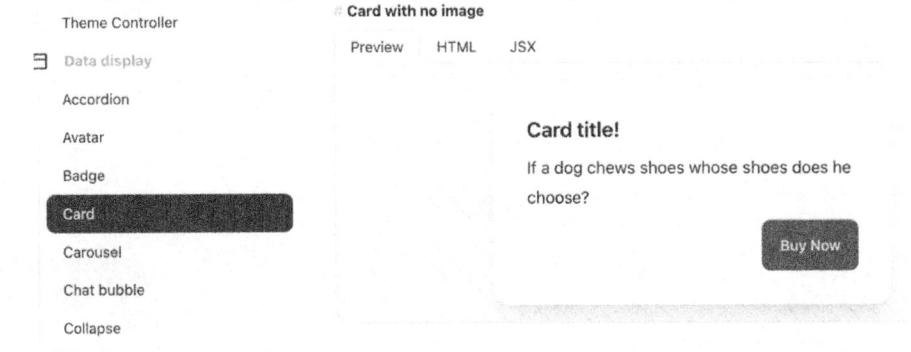

Payment Gateway

Next, we're going to integrate a payment gateway for this screen. We'll be using PayPal as our payment solution because it:
- is available worldwide
- is free to use
- has easy integration

Go to *developer.paypal.com* to get started:

Build Full Stack NextJs AI SAAS

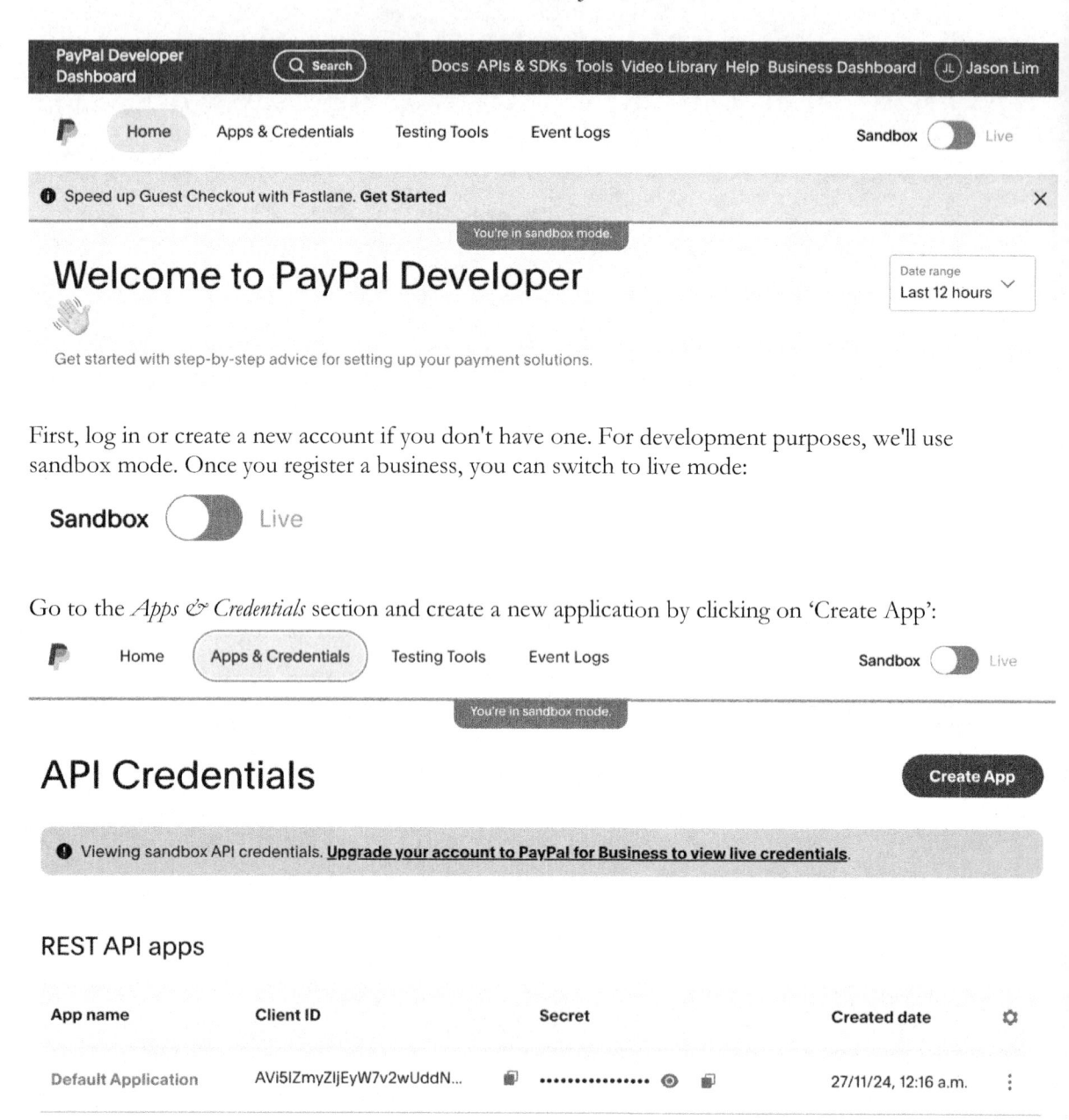

Welcome to PayPal Developer

Get started with step-by-step advice for setting up your payment solutions.

First, log in or create a new account if you don't have one. For development purposes, we'll use sandbox mode. Once you register a business, you can switch to live mode:

Go to the *Apps & Credentials* section and create a new application by clicking on 'Create App':

API Credentials

REST API apps

App name	Client ID	Secret	Created date
Default Application	AVi5IZmyZIjEyW7v2wUddN...	•••••••••••••••	27/11/24, 12:16 a.m.

We will be needing the Client ID later on.

To integrate PayPal, we're going to use the *react-paypal-js* library (*npmjs.com/package/@paypal/react-paypal-js*):

react-paypal-js

React components for the PayPal JS SDK

Install
```
> npm i @paypal/react-paypal-js
```

Repository
github.com/paypal/react-payp...

Run the *npm* command to install:

```
npm i @paypal/react-paypal-js
```

After installation, we need to wrap our application inside the PayPal Script Provider as shown in the documentation:

Usage

This PayPal React library consists of two main parts:

1. Context Provider - this `<PayPalScriptProvider />` component manages loading the JS SDK script. Add it to the root of your React app. It uses the Context API for managing state and communicating to child components. It also supports reloading the script when parameters change.
2. SDK Components - components like `<PayPalButtons />` are used to render the UI for PayPal products served by the JS SDK.

```js
// App.js
import { PayPalScriptProvider, PayPalButtons } from "@paypal/react-paypal-

export default function App() {
    return (
        <PayPalScriptProvider options={{ clientId: "test" }}>
            <PayPalButtons style={{ layout: "horizontal" }} />
        </PayPalScriptProvider>
    );
}
```

In our *provider*.js, we'll wrap our application by adding:

```
"use client"
import React, { useEffect, useState } from 'react'

import { useUser } from '@clerk/nextjs'
import { UserDetailContext } from './_context/UserDetailContext';
import axios from 'axios';
import { PayPalScriptProvider } from '@paypal/react-paypal-js';

function Provider({children}) {

    const {user} = useUser();
    const [userDetail, setUserDetail] = useState([]);

    useEffect(()=>{
        user&&VerifyUser();
    },[user])

    const VerifyUser = async () => {
        const dataResult=await axios.post('/api/verify-user',{
            user:user
        })
        setUserDetail(dataResult.data.result);
    }


  return (
    <UserDetailContext.Provider value={{ userDetail, setUserDetail }}>
      <PayPalScriptProvider options={{ clientId: process.env.NEXT_PUBLIC_PAYPAL_CLIENT_ID }}>
        <div>{children}</div>
      </PayPalScriptProvider>
    </UserDetailContext.Provider>
  )
}

export default Provider
```

In *PayPalScriptProvider*, we need to add our client ID. Go to the *.env* file and add:

```
NEXT_PUBLIC_PAYPAL_CLIENT_ID= your_client_id_here
```

You can get this client ID from your PayPal dashboard:

REST API apps

App name	Client ID
Default Application	AVi5IZmyZIjEyW7v2wUddN...

Adding the Payment Button

Below the purchase options, we want to display the Paypal payment button when a user has made her selection.

Buy More Credits

5 credits	10 credits	25 credits	50 credits	100 credits
for $0.99	for $1.99	for $3.99	for $6.99	for $9.99
Buy	Buy	Buy	Buy	Buy

PayPal — The safer, easier way to pay

To display the PayPal button, the *react-paypal* documentation mentions we need to add the PayPal button:

```
// App.js
import { PayPalScriptProvider, PayPalButtons } from "@paypal/react-paypal-

export default function App() {
    return (
        <PayPalScriptProvider options={{ clientId: "test" }}>
            <PayPalButtons style={{ layout: "horizontal" }} />
        </PayPalScriptProvider>
    );
}
```

So let's go to the *../buy-credits/page*.jsx file, and we will add a *div* with a condition: if user has selected an option, we'll show the payment option. Add in **bold**:

```jsx
...
import { PayPalButtons } from '@paypal/react-paypal-js';

function BuyCredits() {

    const [selectedOption,setSelectedOption]=useState([]);
    const creditsOption=[
      ...
      ]

  return (
    <div>
        <div className="text-2xl font-bold text-center mb-6">
            Buy More Credits
        </div>
        <div className="flex flex-row gap-4 justify-center">
            {creditsOption.map((item,index)=>(
                <div key={index} className="...">
                   ...
                   ...
                </div>
            ))}
        </div>
        <div className="max-w-3xl mx-auto mt-4 px-4">
            {selectedOption?.amount&&
                <PayPalButtons style={{ layout: "horizontal", width: "100%"}}
                />
            }
        </div>
    </div>
  )
}
```

We check if *selectedOption?.amount* exists, meaning user has selected an option, we render the Paypal button.

If we run our application and go to *localhost:3000/dashboard/buy-credits*, select any option and you can see we render the PayPal button:

Buy More Credits

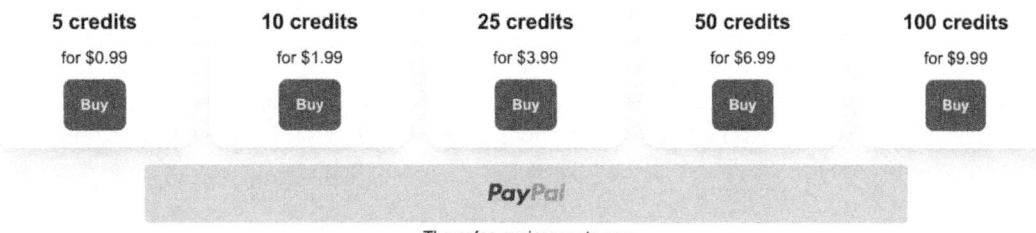

5 credits	10 credits	25 credits	50 credits	100 credits
for $0.99	for $1.99	for $3.99	for $6.99	for $9.99
Buy	Buy	Buy	Buy	Buy

PayPal
The safer, easier way to pay

When you click on PayPal, you'll see all available payment methods. You can either pay with PayPal or use a debit/credit card without creating a PayPal account:

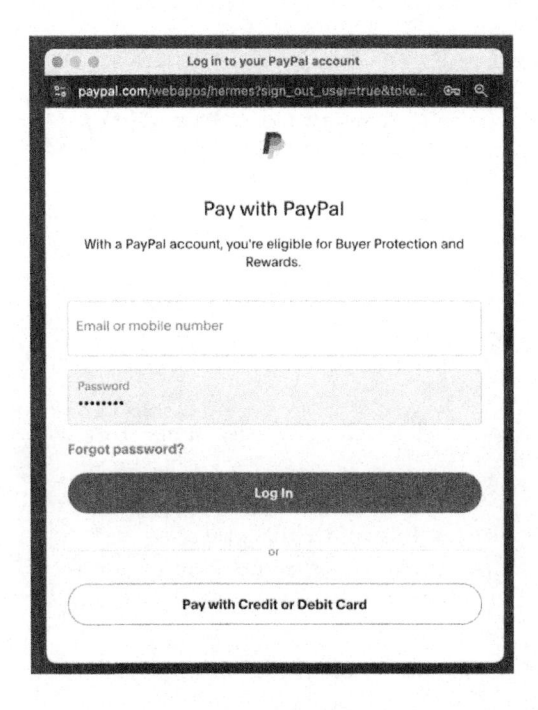

When you log in, you'll be directed to a page displaying the amount and other details. Currently, the amount shows as $0.01:

We haven't provided the selected option's amount yet, but we'll do that shortly. Now, let's customize it further.

Customizing PayPal Payment

To process a payment, you first need to create an order in the PayPal button. In */dashboard/buy-credits/page*.jsx, the Paypal button has a 'createOrder' property that takes an arrow function to handle the purchasing. Add in **bold**:

```
{selectedOption?.amount&&
    <PayPalButtons style={{ layout: "horizontal", width:
      "100%"}}
        createOrder={(data,actions)=>{
            return actions?.order.create({
                purchase_units:[
                    {
                        amount:{
                            value:selectedOption?
                                    .amount?.toFixed(2),
                            currency_code:'USD'
                        }
                    }
                ]
            })
        }}
    />
}
```

First, we need to return 'actions?.order.create'. Within *create()*, we'll specify 'purchase_units'. Inside *purchase_units*, we need to specify *amount*.

For *amount*, we'll use the value *selectedOption?.amount*. We format it to two decimal places using *.toFixed(2))* and also specify the currency code e.g. *USD*. That completes the order creation process.

Let's save and test these changes. In *localhost:3000/dashboard/buy-credits*, when you click on PayPal and pay, instead of showing $0.01, it should display the correct amount that we selected:

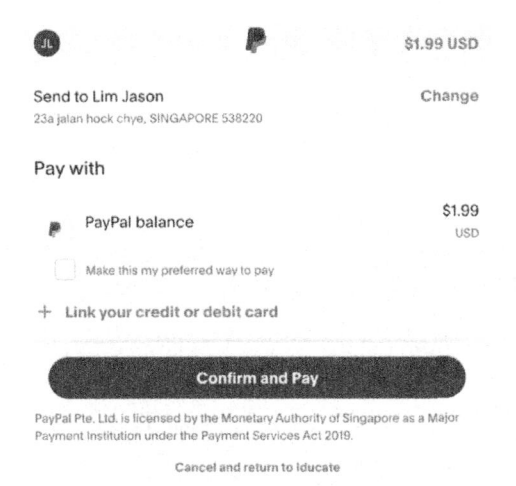

Handle Payment Success

Next, we need to handle the payment approval. Add an 'onApprove' handler that will call our 'onPaymentSuccess' method when the payment is completed:

```
function BuyCredits() {
    ...
    const creditsOption=[
        ...
    ]

    const onPaymentSuccess=async()=>{
        console.log("payment Success...")
    }
...
...
            {selectedOption?.amount&&
                <PayPalButtons style={{ layout: "horizontal", width: "100%"}}
                    onApprove={()=>onPaymentSuccess()}
                    onCancel={()=>console.log("Payment Cancelled")}
                    createOrder={(data,actions)=>{
                        return actions?.order.create({
                            ...
                        })
                    }}
                />
    }
```

`onPaymentSuccess` will be called only when the payment is successful. For now, we just *console.log("payment success")*.

For handling payment cancellation or failure, we add an 'onCancel' handler that logs a 'payment cancelled' message.

Let's test our app. Trying purchasing an option using PayPal's test card numbers, which you can find by searching for 'PayPal test cards' on Google or going to: *developer.paypal.com/tools/sandbox/card-testing/*

Under 'Card Testing', you can generate test cards from different countries (you're not limited to US cards). Select a card type e.g. Visa. Simply click 'Generate' and it will create a test card number for you:

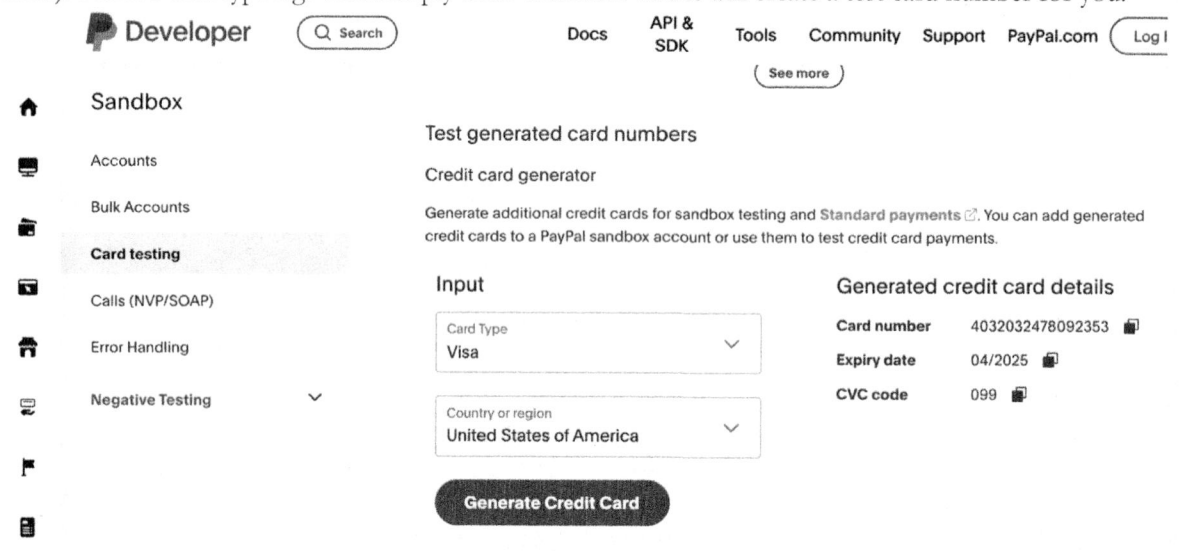

Let's proceed with making a payment to test if everything is working. Select an option and click PayPal. Choose the 'debit or credit card' option and enter the test card details.

Click 'Pay Now' and follow up with the other prompts. And when done, if you check the browser's console, you'll see the 'payment success' message logged:

```
payment                page.jsx:33
Success...
>
```

This confirms that after a successful payment, the code executed our callback method and logged the message to the console. That completes the basic payment setup.

Update User's Credits in Database after Payment

Next, we'll update the user's credits in the database after a successful payment. We'll add database integration to update the user's credits. In *../buy-credits/page*.jsx, add in **bold**:

```
...
import React, {useState, useContext } from 'react'
import { db } from '../../../config/db';
import { Users } from '../../../config/schema';
import { UserDetailContext } from '../../_context/UserDetailContext';

function BuyCredits() {

    const [selectedOption,setSelectedOption]=useState([]);
    const {userDetail,setUserDetail}=useContext(UserDetailContext);
   ...
   ...

   const onPaymentSuccess=async()=>{
       console.log("payment Success...")
       const result=await db.update(Users)
         .set({
             credits:userDetail?.credits+selectedOption?.credits
         }).returning({id:Users.id});
   }
```

Code Explanation

To get the current credits, we'll use the user context.

```
    const {userDetail,setUserDetail}=useContext(UserDetailContext);
```

We destructure 'userDetail' from our context using 'useContext(UserDetailContext)'. Remember that we have setup the *UserDetailContext* in our *provider*.js:

```
function Provider({children}) {
  ...
  return (
    <UserDetailContext.Provider value={{ userDetail, setUserDetail }}>
      <PayPalScriptProvider options={{ clientId: ... }}>
        <div>{children}</div>
      </PayPalScriptProvider>
    </UserDetailContext.Provider>
  )
}
```

We call '*await db.update(Users)*' to modify the *User* schema. We'll use '*.set*' to update the *credits* field:

```
const result=await db.update(Users)
  .set({
      credits:userDetail?.credits+selectedOption?.credits
  }).returning({id:Users.id});
```

We add to the existing credits using '*userDetail?.credit*' plus the credit amount from '*selectedOption?.credit*'. After updating the credits, we'll return the user's ID. That completes our update logic.

Redirect User to Dashboard Upon Success

Next, when we get a successful result, we want to redirect the user to the dashboard. Add in **bold**:

```
...
import { useRouter } from 'next/navigation';

function BuyCredits() {

  const [selectedOption,setSelectedOption]=useState([]);
  const {userDetail,setUserDetail}=useContext(UserDetailContext);
  const router=useRouter();

  const onPaymentSuccess=async()=>{
      console.log("payment Success...")
      const result=await db.update(Users)
        .set({
            credits:userDetail?.credits+selectedOption?.credits
        }).returning({id:Users.id});

    if(result)
        {
            router.push('/dashboard');
        }
  }
...
```

Code Explanation

```
import { useRouter } from 'next/navigation';

function BuyCredits() {
  ...
  const router=useRouter();
```

We use the 'useRouter' hook from '`next/navigation`'.

```
if(result)
    {
        router.push('/dashboard');
    }
```

And if the update is successful, we then call '*router.push*' to navigate to the dashboard page.

Running our App

Let's test our changes. Before you proceed, it would be advisable to log out and log in from the app again, to ensure a fresh start (and ensure the user credit are captured correctly in the browser cache).

Select any amount, click PayPal, and choose the debit/credit card option. Enter the card details and click 'Pay Now'. After updating the address, you'll be redirected to the dashboard.

Currently, you need to refresh to see your credits update from 5 to 30. To avoid this refresh requirement, we can update the User Detail context immediately after the payment. Add in **bold**:

```
if(result)
    {
        setUserDetail(prev=>({
            ...prev,
            credits:userDetail?.credits+selectedOption?.credits
        }))
        router.push('/dashboard');
    }
```

We use a spread operator '…' to keep all previous values (*...prev*), then update the credits field with the new amount.

With this context update, you'll see the changes instantly without refreshing. You now have the new credits available for creating interiors.

Deduct One Credit from Account

We need to deduct one credit from the account whenever you generate a design. Let's go to the *../create-new/page*.jsx. In the *generateAiImage* function, we add a call to a new method:

```
const generateAIImage = async () => {
    ...
    const result = await axios.post('/api/interior-ai', {
    ...
    });

    setAiOutputImage(result.data.result)
    await updateUserCredits();

    setOpenOutputDialog(true);
    setLoading(false);
}
```

After generating the image, we have a *updateUserCredits* method to handle credit deduction. Add:

```
...
import React, {useState, useContext} from 'react'
import { db } from '../../../config/db'
import { Users } from '../../../config/schema'
import { UserDetailContext } from '../../_context/UserDetailContext';

function CreateNew() {
    ...
    ...
    const [orgImage,setOrgImage]=useState();
    const {userDetail,setUserDetail}=useContext(UserDetailContext);

    ...
    const updateUserCredits=async()=>{
        const result=await db.update(Users).set({
          credits:userDetail?.credits-1
        }).returning({id:Users.id});

        if(result)
        {
            setUserDetail(prev=>({
              ...prev,
              credits:userDetail?.credits-1
        }))
            return result[0].id
        }
    }
```

When a user generates an image, we'll deduct one credit from their total

We first call 'await db.update' to modify the *User* schema. We set *credits* to *userDetail?.credits* – 1. For the return value, we'll return the ID (this is optional and can be customized based on your needs).

If the result is true, update the *userDetail* context using the same technique we discussed earlier. Then return just *result[0].id*.

To test this, let's try generating a room and if you return to the home screen, you'll notice the credits have reduced by 1.

Chapter 12: Deploy App

Now let's deploy this application to the cloud, making it a true SaaS (Software as a Service) that can be offered to users. I've added a simple yet beautiful landing screen to the application:

The code for this landing screen is placed in /*dashboard*/*page*.js (you can get the source code from suppor@i-ducate.com):

```
import Image from "next/image";
import Link from "next/link";

import React from 'react'

export default function Home() {
  return (
    <div>
      <div className="hero min-h-screen bg-base-200">
        <div className="hero-content text-center">
          <div className="max-w-[85rem]">
            {/* Main Title */}
            <div className="mb-8">
              <h1 className="text-5xl font-bold mb-4">
```

```jsx
          AI Room and Home
          <span className="text-primary"> Interior AI</span>
        </h1>
        <p className="text-lg">
          Transform Your Space with AI
        </p>
      </div>

      {/* Get Started Button */}
      <div className="flex justify-center mb--8">
        <Link href="/dashboard" className="btn btn-primary gap-2">
          Get started
        </Link>
      </div>

      {/* Main Image */}
      <div className="flex justify-center mb-16">
        <Image src={'/group.png'} alt="mockup" width={1000} height={600} />
      </div>
     </div>
    </div>
   </div>
  </div>
 );
}
```

For cloud deployment, we'll use Vercel - a cloud service provider that's specifically optimized for Next.js applications. Our deployment process will involve:
- Pushing our code to GitHub
- Deploying from GitHub to Vercel

Let's first begin the deployment process. First, initialize Git in the Terminal by running (in your project folder): `git init`

After initializing Git, let's create a new repository on GitHub:

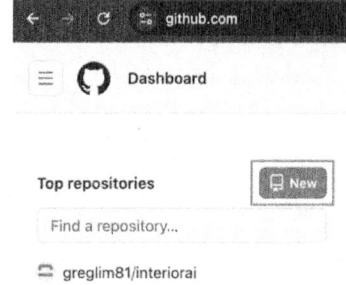

Click on 'New' and give your repository a name e.g. 'interior-ai':

Create a new repository

A repository contains all project files, including the revisi elsewhere? Import a repository.

Required fields are marked with an asterisk (*).

Repository template

No template ▼

Start your repository with a template repository's contents.

Owner *   **Repository name ***

greglim81 ▼ / interior-ai

✓ interior-ai is available.

Choose whether you want it to be public or private, then click 'Create Repository':

Public
Anyone on the internet can see this repository. You choose who can commit.

Private
You choose who can see and commit to this repository.

After creating the repository, add the remote origin by copying and pasting the provided URL command in the Terminal:

...or push an existing repository from the command line

```
git remote add origin https://github.com/greglim81/interior-ai.git
git branch -M main
git push -u origin main
```

This command sets your remote origin, telling the Terminal where to push your code repository. Next, run '*git add* .' to stage all your files for commitment to GitHub:

`git add .`

Create your first commit by running:

`git commit -m "initial commit"`

For the first push to your repository, use:

```
git push -u origin main
```

After this initial push, you can simply use 'git push' for future updates.

Once you've initiated the push, wait for the process to complete. After it finishes, refresh your GitHub page and you'll see your code in the repository:

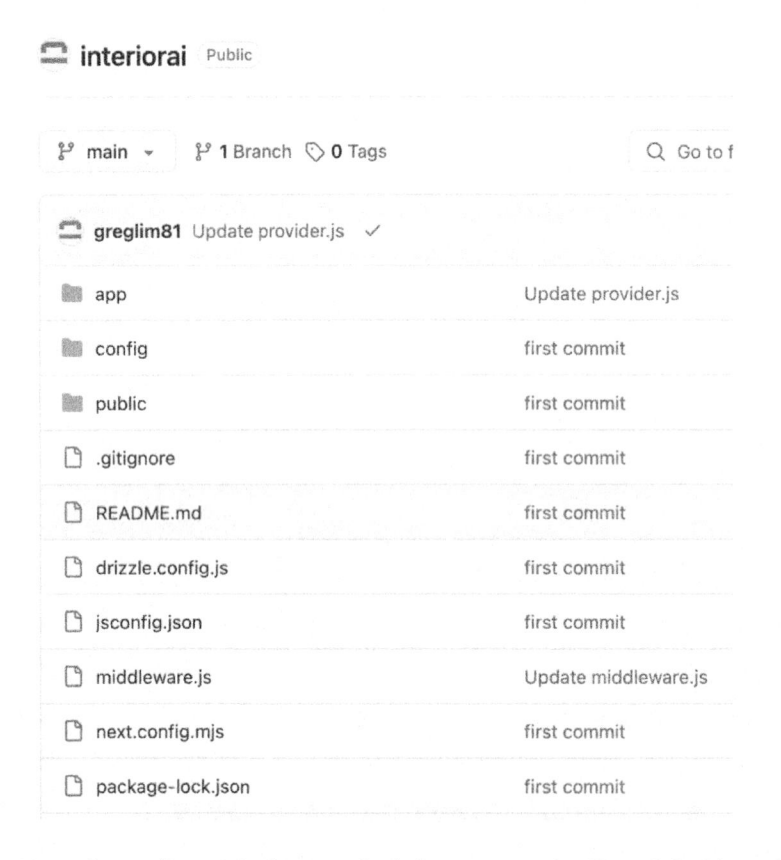

```
interiorai  Public

main ▾    1 Branch   0 Tags                              Go to f

greglim81  Update provider.js  ✓

app                              Update provider.js
config                           first commit
public                           first commit
.gitignore                       first commit
README.md                        first commit
drizzle.config.js                first commit
jsconfig.json                    first commit
middleware.js                    Update middleware.js
next.config.mjs                  first commit
package-lock.json                first commit
```

Now that we've pushed our code, let's return to the Vercel dashboard (vercel.com). You'll see a view similar to this one, which shows all deployed projects:

Build Full Stack NextJs AI SAAS

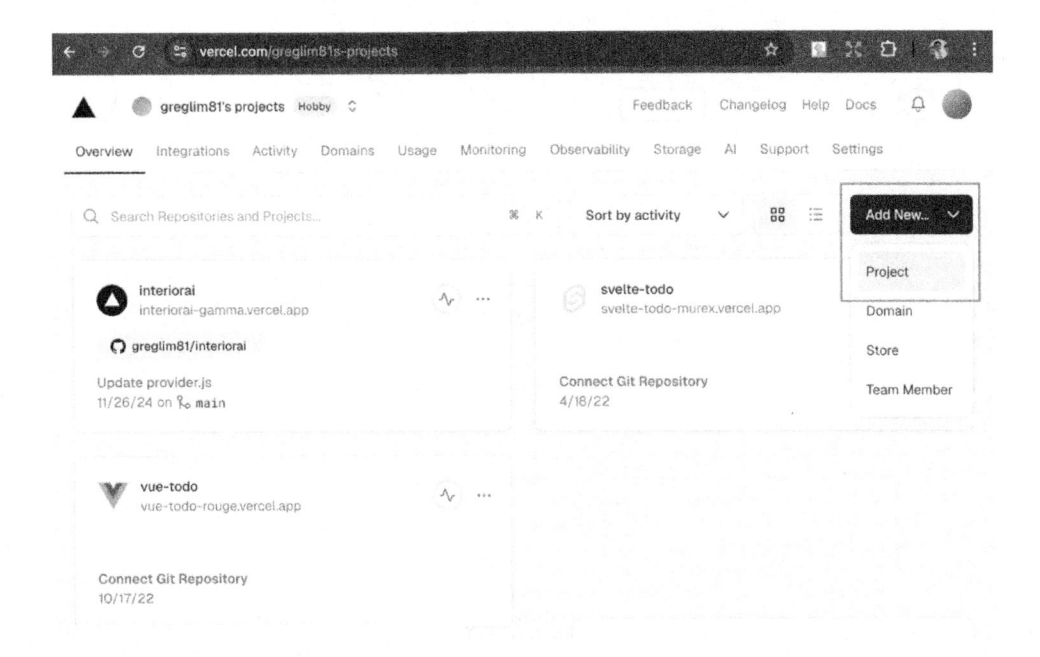

Click 'Add New' to begin deploying your project.

Select 'Project' and connect your GitHub repository. You can also connect repositories from GitLab or Bitbucket. Once connected, you'll see your recently pushed project - simply click 'Import' to proceed."

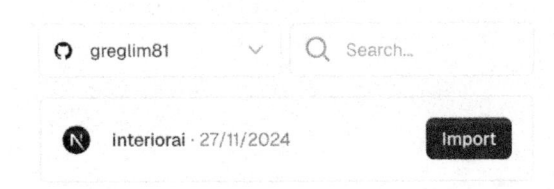

After importing, enter your project name. Vercel will automatically detect that you're using Next.js:

New Project

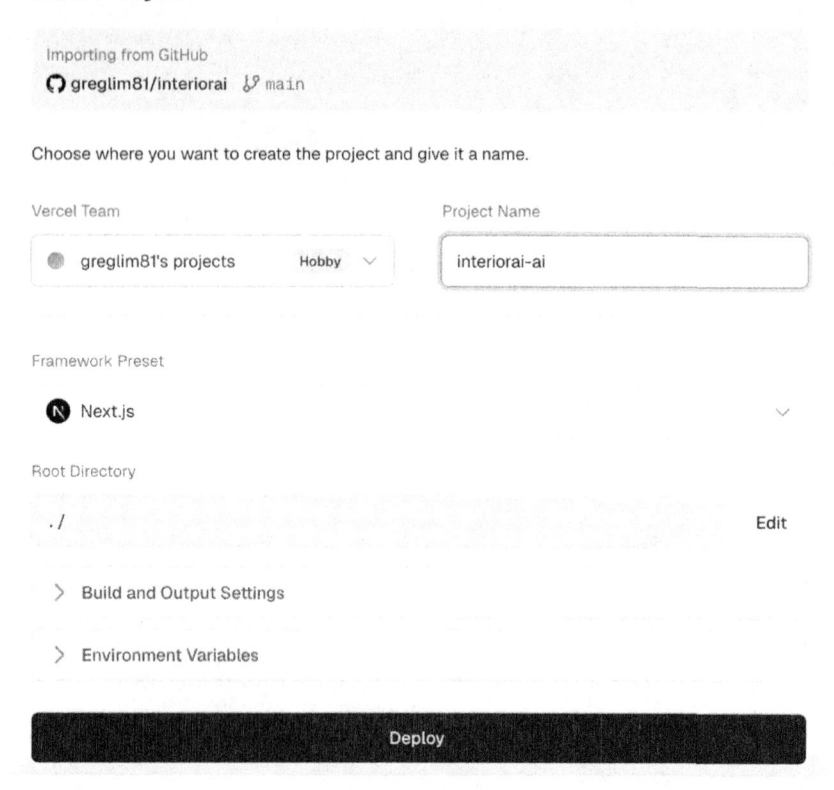

Importing from GitHub
greglim81/interiorai — main

Choose where you want to create the project and give it a name.

Vercel Team: greglim81's projects (Hobby)

Project Name: interiorai-ai

Framework Preset: Next.js

Root Directory: ./   Edit

> Build and Output Settings

> Environment Variables

Deploy

Leave the default framework settings unchanged. However, you need to add your environment variables to Vercel. Copy all the variables from your *.env* file and paste them here:

Environment Variables

Key	Value
EXAMPLE_NAME	I9JU23NF394R6HH
NEXT_PUBLIC_DATABASE_URL	postgresql://neondb_owner:XO0nGa4bJ\
NEXT_PUBLIC_CLERK_PUBLISHABLE_	pk_test_cmVhZHktZmxlYS0xNy5jbGVyay
CLERK_SECRET_KEY	sk_test_lGngNsRkuzPktIofOT23XrwLgnd
NEXT_PUBLIC_CLERK_SIGN_IN_URL	/sign-in
NEXT_PUBLIC_CLERK_SIGN_UP_URL	/sign-up
NEXT_PUBLIC_REPLICATE_API_TOKEN	r8_F9Hq9hMACHUUCsoj3xxDuZviJsXr9T
NEXT_PUBLIC_PAYPAL_CLIENT_ID	AVi5lZmyZljEyW7v2wUddN_7GG3_FbOB(

+ Add More

Tip: Paste an .env above to populate the form. Learn more

Vercel will automatically detect the keys and their corresponding values.

Click 'Deploy' to start the process:

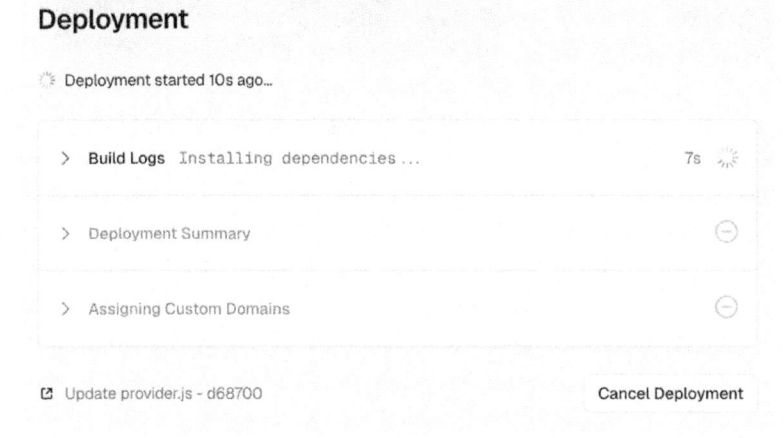

Deployment

Deployment started 10s ago...

> Build Logs Installing dependencies...   7s

> Deployment Summary

> Assigning Custom Domains

Update provider.js - d68700   Cancel Deployment

Deploying your application to the cloud is this straightforward. The deployment process includes:

- Building logs
- Installing dependencies
- Building and deploying your application

Once complete, you'll see a successful deployment confirmation. Click 'Continue to Dashboard' to view your application's domain:

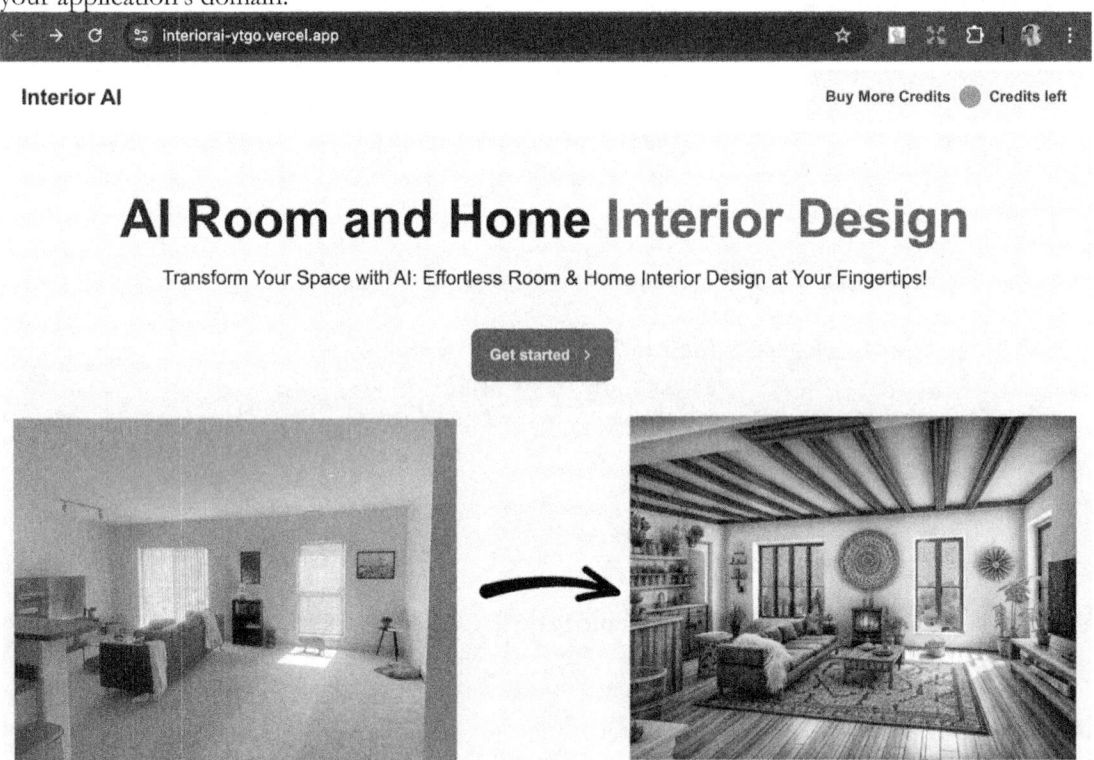

Congratulations! Your application is now live and accessible online! Click 'Get Started' and log in to explore the full functionality. The room design feature and all other components work seamlessly, requiring no additional configuration.

Final Words

We have gone through quite a lot of content to equip you with the skills to create your own AI Saas apps.

Hopefully, you have enjoyed this book and would like to learn more from me. I would love to get your feedback, learning what you liked and didn't for us to improve.

Please feel free to email me at support@i-ducate.com to get updated versions of this book.

If you didn't like the book, or if you feel that I should have covered certain additional topics, please email us to let us know. This book can only get better thanks to readers like you.

If you like the book, I would appreciate if you could leave us a review too. Thank you and all the best for your learning journey!

About the Author

Greg Lim is a technologist and author of several programming books. Greg has many years in teaching programming in tertiary institutions and he places special emphasis on learning by doing.

Contact Greg at support@i-ducate.com

Printed in Great Britain
by Amazon